Berlitz

5464 2318

Mexican
Spanish

phrase book & dictionary

Ricos

Huaraches
con
carne asada

RICAS
ENCHILADAS
SUIZAS

Parrillada
MIXTA
2 PERSONAS

TACOS AL PASTOR
ASADA

Berlitz Publishing
New York   London   Singapore

Contacting the Editors
Every effort has been made to provide accurate information in this publication, but changes are inevitable. The publisher cannot be responsible for any resulting loss, inconvenience or injury. We would appreciate it if readers would call our attention to any errors or outdated information. We also welcome your suggestions; if you come across a relevant expression not in our phrase book, please contact us at: **comments@berlitzpublishing.com**

Eleventh Printing: January 2014
Printed in China

Senior Commissioning Editor: Kate Drynan
Design: Beverley Speight
Translation: updated by Wordbank
Production Manager: Vicky Glover
Picture Researcher: Beverley Speight
Cover Photos: © APA Anna Mockford & Nick Bonetti; istockphoto

Interior Photos: All APA Anna Mockford & Nick Bonetti except istockphoto p.14,65,6 9,121,139,148,153,154,157,159,161; APA Britta Jaschinski p.16,67; APA Bev Speight p.21,44,128,140,145,174; APA David Midgley p.108.

Contents

Pronunciation	7	Vowels	9
Consonants	7	How to use this Book	10

Survival

Arrival & Departure	**13**	Breakdown & Repair	35
ESSENTIAL	13	Accidents	36
Border Control	13		
		Places to Stay	**37**
Money	**15**	ESSENTIAL	37
ESSENTIAL	15	Somewhere to Stay	38
At the Bank	16	At the Hotel	39
		Price	40
Getting Around	**18**	Preferences	41
ESSENTIAL	18	Questions	42
Tickets	19	Problems	43
Plane	20	Checking Out	44
Checking In	22	Renting	45
Luggage	22	Domestic Items	45
Finding your Way	23	At the Hostel	46
Train	24	Going Camping	47
Departures	25		
On Board	25	**Communications**	**48**
Bus	26	ESSENTIAL	48
Metro	27	Online	49
Boat & Ferry	28	Social Media	50
Taxi	29	Phone	50
Bicycle & Motorbike	31	Telephone Etiquette	52
Car Hire	31	Fax	54
Fuel Station	32	Post	54
Asking Directions	33		
Parking	35		

Food & Drink

Eating Out 57
ESSENTIAL 57
Where to Eat 58
Reservations & Preferences 58
How to Order 60
Cooking Methods 61
Dietary Requirements 62
Dining with Children 63
How to Complain 64
Paying 64

Meals & Cooking 66
Breakfast 66
Appetizers 67
Soup 68
Fish & Seafood 69
Meat & Poultry 71

Vegetables & Staples 73
Fruit 74
Dessert 76
Cheese 77
Sauces & Condiments 77
At the Market 78
In the Kitchen 80

Drinks 81
ESSENTIAL 81
Non-alcoholic Drinks 82
Apéritifs, Cocktails & Liqueurs 84
Beer 84
Wine 84

On the Menu 85

People

Conversation 99
ESSENTIAL 99
Language Difficulties 100
Making Friends 101
Travel Talk 102
Personal 102
Work & School 103
Weather 104

Romance 105
ESSENTIAL 105
The Dating Game 105
Accepting & Rejecting 106
Getting Intimate 107
Sexual Preferences 107

Leisure Time

Sightseeing   **109**
ESSENTIAL   109
Tourist Information   109
On Tour   110
Seeing the Sights   111
Religious Sites   113

Shopping   **114**
ESSENTIAL   114
At the Shops   114
Ask an Assistant   116
Personal Preferences   117
Paying & Bargaining   118
Making a Complaint   120
Services   120
Hair & Beauty   120
Antiques   122
Clothing   122
Colors   124

Clothes & Accessories   124
Fabric   125
Shoes   126
Sizes   127
Newsagent & Tobacconist   127
Photography   128
Souvenirs   129

Sport & Leisure   **131**
ESSENTIAL   131
Watching Sport   132
Playing Sport   132
At the Beach/Pool   133
Out in the Country   135

Going Out   **137**
ESSENTIAL   137
Entertainment   137
Nightlife   138

Special Requirements

Business Travel   **141**
ESSENTIAL   141
On Business   141

Traveling with Children   **143**
ESSENTIAL   143
Out & About   143

Baby Essentials   144
Babysitting   145
Health & Emergency   146

Disabled Travelers   **146**
ESSENTIAL   146
Asking for Assistance   147

In an Emergency

Emergencies **149**
ESSENTIAL 149

Police **150**
ESSENTIAL 150
Crime & Lost Property 151

Health **152**
ESSENTIAL 152
Finding a Doctor 152
Symptoms 152
Conditions 154
Treatment 155
Hospital 155
Dentist 156
Gynecologist 156
Optician 157
Payment & Insurance 157
Pharmacy 158
ESSENTIAL 158
What to Take 158

Basic Supplies 160

The Basics **162**
Grammar 162
Numbers 167
ESSENTIAL 167
Ordinal Numbers 168
Time 169
ESSENTIAL 169
Days 169
ESSENTIAL 169
Dates 170
Months 170
Seasons 170
Holidays 171
Conversion Tables 171
Kilometers to Miles Conversions 172
Measurement 172
Temperature 172
Oven Temperature 172

Dictionary

English-Mexican Spanish 174
Dictionary

Mexican Spanish-English 200
Dictionary

Pronunciation

This section is designed to make you familiar with the sounds of Mexican Spanish using our simplified phonetic transcription. You'll find the pronunciation of the Spanish letters and sounds explained below, together with their "imitated" equivalents. This system is used throughout the phrase book; simply read the pronunciation as if it were English, noting any special rules below. Underlined letters indicate that that syllable should be stressed. The **acute accent** ´ indicates stress, e.g. **río**, *rree·oh*. Some Spanish words have more than one meaning. In these instances, the accent mark is also used to distinguish between them, e.g.: **él (he)** and **el (the)**; **sí (yes)** and **si (if)**. There are some differences in vocabulary and pronunciation between the Spanish spoken in Spain and that in the Americas—although each is easily understood by the other. This phrase book and dictionary is specifically geared to travelers in Mexico.

Consonants

Letter	Approximate Pronunciation	Symbol	Example	Pronunciation
b	1. as in English	**b**	bueno	*bweh·noh*
	2. between vowels as in English, but softer	**b**	bebida	*beh·bee·dah*
c	1. before e and **i** like **s** in same	**s**	centro	*sehn·troh*
	2. otherwise like **k** in kit	**k**	como	*koh·moh*
ch	as in English	**ch**	mucho	*moo·choh*
g	1. before **e** and **i**, like **ch** in Scottish loch	**kh**	urgente	*oor·khehn·teh*
	2. otherwise, like **g** in get	**g**	ninguno	*neen·goo·noh*

Letter	Approximate Pronunciation	Symbol	Example	Pronunciation
h	always silent		hombre	*ohm•breh*
j	like **ch** in Scottish loch	**kh**	bajo	*bah•khoh*
ll	like y in yellow	**y**	lleno	*yeh•noh*
ñ	like ni in onion	**ny**	señor	*seh•nyohr*
q	like k in kick	**k**	quince	*keen•seh*
r	1. at the beginning of a word or after **n**, **l** or **s**, strongly trilled	**rr**	río	*rree•oh*
	2. otherwise, softly trilled	**r**	marzo	*mahr•soh*
rr	strongly trilled	**rr**	arriba	*ah•rree•bah*
s	1. like s in same	**s**	sus	*soos*
	2. before **b, d, g, l, m, n**, like s in rose	**z**	mismo	*meez•moh*
v	like **b** in bad, but softer	**b**	viejo	*beeyeh•khoh*
x	1. at the beginning of a word, like **s** in same or like **ch** in Scottish loch	**s, kh**	Xochimilco, xilófono	*soh•chee•meel•koh* *khee•loh•foh•noh*
	2. in some words of Aztec origin, like **ch** in Scottish loch	**kh**	México	*meh•khee•coh*
	3. otherwise as in English	**x**	exámen	*eh•xah•mehn*
z	like **s** in same	**s**	brazo	*brah•soh*

Letters **d, f, k, l, m, n, p, t, w** and **y** are pronounced as in English.

Vowels

Letter	Approximate Pronunciation	Symbol	Example	Pronunciation
a	like the **a** in father	**ah**	gracias	*grah•seeyahs*
e	like **e** in get	**eh**	esta	*ehs•tah*
i	like **ee** in meet	**ee**	sí	*see*
o	like **o** in rope	**oh**	dos	*dohs*
u	1. like **oo** in food	**oo**	uno	*oo•noh*
	2. silent after **g** and **q**		que	*keh*
	3. when marked **ü,** like w in well	**w**	agüero	*ah•gweh•roh*
y	1. like **y** in yellow	**y**	hoy	*oy*
	2. when alone, like **ee** in meet	**ee**	y	*ee*
	3. when preceded by an **a**, sounds like **y + ee**, with **ee** faintly pronounced	**aye**	hay	*aye*

How to use this Book

Sometimes you see two alternatives separated by a slash. Choose the one that's right for your situation.

ESSENTIAL

I'm on vacation/business.

Estoy aquí de vacaciones/en viaje de negocios. ehs·toy ah·kee deh bah·kah·seeyoh·nehs/ehn beeyah·kheh deh neh·goh·seeyohs

I'm going to...

Voy a... boy ah...

I'm staying at the...Hotel.

Me alojo en el Hotel.... meh ah·loh·khoh ehn ehl oh·tehl...

Words you may see are shown in YOU MAY SEE boxes.

YOU MAY SEE...

ADUANA	customs
ARTÍCULOS LIBRES DE IMPUESTOS	duty-free goods
ARTÍCULOS QUE DECLARAR	goods to declare

Any of the words or phrases listed can be plugged into the sentence below.

Tickets

A...ticket.	**Un boleto...** oon boh·leh·toh...
one-way	**sencillo** sehn·see·yoh
round-trip [return]	**redondo** rreh·dohn·doh
first class	**de primera clase** deh pree·meh·rah klah·seh
economy class	**clase turista** klah·seh tuh·rees·tah

Mexican Spanish phrases appear in purple.

Read the simplified pronunciation as if it were English. For more on pronunciation, see page 7.

Making Friends

What's your name?
I'd like to introduce you to...
Pleased to meet you.

¿Cómo te llamas? *koh·moh teh yah·mahs*
Quiero presentarle a...
keeyeh·roh preh·sehn·tahr·leh ah...
Encantado *m* **/Encantada** *f* **.**
ehn·kahn·tah·doh/ehn·kahn·tah·dah

For Communications, see page 40.

Related phrases can be found by going to the page number indicated.

When different gender forms apply, the masculine form is followed by *m*; feminine by *f*.

In Mexican Spanish, there are a number of forms for 'you' taking different verb forms: **tú** (singular, informal), **usted** (singular, formal) and **ustedes** (plural).

Information boxes contain relevant country, culture and language tips.

Expressions you may hear are shown in You May Hear boxes.

YOU MAY HEAR...

Hablo muy poco inglés.
ah·bloh mooy poh·koh een·glehs

I only speak a little English.

Color-coded side bars identify each section of the book.

Survival

Arrival & Departure   13
Money   15
Getting Around   18
Places to Stay   37
Communications   48

ESSENTIAL

I'm here on vacation [holiday]/business.	**Estoy aquí de vacaciones/en viaje de negocios.** *ehs·toy ah·kee deh bah·kah·seeyoh·nehs/ehn beeyah·kheh deh neh·goh·seeyohs*
I'm going to...	**Voy a...** *boy ah...*
I'm staying at the...Hotel.	**Me alojo en el Hotel...** *meh ah·loh·khoh ehn ehl oh·tehl...*

YOU MAY HEAR...

Su pasaporte, por favor.
soo pah·sah·pohr·teh pohr fah·bohr
Your passport, please.

¿Cuál es el propósito de su visita?
kwahl ehs ehl proh·poh·see·toh deh soo bee·see·tah
What's the purpose of your visit?

¿Dónde se aloja?
dohn·deh seh ah·loh·khah
Where are you staying?

¿Cuánto tiempo piensa quedarse?
kwahn·toh teeyehm·poh peeyehn·sah keh·dar·seh
How long are you staying?

¿Con quién viaja?
kohn keeyehn beeyah·khah
Who are you here with?

Border Control

I'm just passing through.	**Estoy de paso.** *ehs·toy deh pah·soh*
I'd like to declare...	**Quiero declarar...** *keeyeh·roh deh·klah·rahr...*
I have nothing to declare.	**No tengo nada que declarar.** *noh tehn·goh nah·dah keh deh·klah·rahr*

To enter Mexico, you must present a completed **Customs Declaration Form.** Items destined for personal use don't need to be declared. However, the value of any other items brought into the country do. Limits vary depending on whether you enter Mexico by air, sea or land. Incorrectly reporting the value of an item or not declaring an item may be penalized by fines and/or possible confiscation.

YOU MAY HEAR...

¿Tiene algo que declarar?
teeyeh·neh ahl·goh keh deh·klah·rahr

Anything to declare?

Tiene que pagar impuestos por esto.
teeyeh·neh keh pah·gahr eem·pwehs·tohs pohr ehs·toh

You must pay duty.

Abra esta maleta.
ah·brah ehs·tah mah·leh·tah

Open this bag

YOU MAY SEE…

ADUANA	customs
ARTÍCULOS LIBRES DE IMPUESTOS	duty-free goods
ARTÍCULOS QUE DECLARAR	goods to declare
NADA QUE DECLARAR	nothing to declare
CONTROL DE PASAPORTES	passport control
POLICÍA	police

15

Money

ESSENTIAL

Where's…?	**¿Dónde está…?** *dohn•deh ehs•tah…*
the ATM	**el cajero automático**
	ehl kah•kheh•roh aw•toh•mah•tee•koh
the bank	**el banco**
	ehl bahn•koh
the currency	**la casa de cambio**
exchange office	*lah kah•sah deh kahm•beeyoh*
When does the	**¿A qué hora abre/cierra el banco?**
bank open/close?	*ah keh oh•rah ah•breh/seeyeh•rrah ehl bahn•koh*
I'd like to change some	**Quiero cambiar dólares/libras a pesos.**
dollars/pounds	*keeyeh•roh kahm•beeyahr doh•lah•rehs/lee•brahs ah*
into pesos.	*peh•sohs*
I want to cash some	**Quiero cobrar cheques de viajero.**
traveler's checks	*keeyeh•roh koh•brahr cheh•kehs deh*
[cheques].	*beeyah•kheh•roh*

At the Bank

I'd like to change money/get a cash advance.	**Quiero cambiar dinero/un adelanto.** *keeyeh•roh kahm•beeyahr dee•neh•roh/oon ahdeh•lahn•to*
What's the exchange rate/fee?	**¿Cuál es el tipo de cambio?** *kwahl ehs ehl tee•poh deh kahm•beeyoh /* **¿Cuánto es la comisión?** *kwahn•toh ehs lah koh•mee•seeyohn?*
I think there's a mistake.	**Creo que hay un error.** *Krehoh keh ay oon ehrrohr*
I lost my traveler's cheques.	**Perdí mis cheques de viajero.** *pehr•dee mees cheh•kehs deh beeyah•kheh•roh*
My card…	
was lost	**Perdí mí tarjeta.** *pehr•dee mee tahr•kheh•tah*
was stolen	**Me robaron la tarjeta.** *meh rroh•bah•rohn lah tahr•kheh•tah*
doesn't work	**Mi tarjeta no funciona.** *mee tahr•kheh•tah noh foon•seeyoh•nah*
The ATM ate my card.	**El cajero automático se tragó mi tarjeta.** *Ehl kah•heh•ro auto•mah•tico seh tra•goh mee tar•kheh•tah*

Instructions on **ATM machines** are usually given in Spanish. However, those located at international airports and major tourist destinations will most likely have English-language instructions and may even dispense U.S. dollars. Note that while debit cards are readily accepted in most places, many convenience stores may only accept cash. The best rates for exchanging money are usually the banks.

YOU MAY SEE...

INTRODUCIR TARJETA AQUÍ	insert card here
CANCELAR	cancel
BORRAR	clear
INTRODUCIR	enter
NIP	PIN
RETIRAR FONDOS	withdraw
DE CUENTA DE CHEQUES	from checking [current] account
DE CUENTA DE AHORROS	from savings account
COMPROBANTE	receipt

Getting Around

ESSENTIAL

How do I get to town?	**¿Cómo se llega a la ciudad?**
	koh·moh seh yeh·gah ah lah seew·dahd
Where's...?	**¿Dónde está...?** *dohn·deh ehs·tah...*
the airport	**el aeropuerto** *ehl ah·eh·roh·pwehr·toh*
the train station	**la estación del tren** *lah ehs·tah·seeyohn dehl trehn*
the bus station	**la estación de camiones**
	lah ehs·tah·seeyohn deh kah·meeyoh·nehs
the subway [underground]	**la estación del metro** *lah ehs·tah·seeyohn*
How far is it?	**¿A qué distancia está?** *ah keh dees·tahn·seeyah ehs·tah*
Where do I buy a ticket?	**¿Dónde puedo comprar el boleto?** *dohn·deh pweh·doh kohm·prahr ehl*
A one-way/ return-trip ticket to...	**Un boleto sencillo/redondo a...** *oon boh·leh·toh sehn·see·yoh/rreh·dohn·doh ah...*
How much?	**¿Cuánto es?** *kwahn·toh ehs*
Which gate/line/ platform?	**¿Cuál puerta de embarque/ línea andén?** *kwahl pwehr·tah deh ehm·bahr·keh/ lee·neh·ah/ ahn·dehn*
Where can I get a taxi?	**¿Dónde puedo tomar un taxi?** *dohn·deh pweh·doh toh·mahr oon tah·xee*
Take me to this address.	**Lléveme a esta dirección.** *yeh·beh·meh ah ehs·tah dee·rehk·seeyohn*
Where's the car rental [hire]?	**¿Dónde está la renta de autos?** *dohn·deh ehs·ta lah rrehn·tah deh aw·tohs*
Can I have a map?	**¿Puede darme un mapa?** *pweh·deh dahr·meh oon mah·pah*

Tickets

When's...to Acapulco? **¿Cuándo sale...a Acapulco?**
kwahn•doh sah•leh...ah ah•kah•pool•koh

the (first) bus	**el (primer) camión** *ehl (pree•mehr) kah•meeyohn*
the (next) flight	**el (siguiente) vuelo** *ehl (see•geeyehn•teh) bweh•loh*
the (last) train	**el (último) tren** *ehl (ool•tee•moh) trehn*

Where do I buy **¿Dónde puedo comprar el boleto?**
a ticket? *dohn•deh pweh•doh kohm•prahr ehl boh•leh•toh*

One/ Two ticket(s) **Un/Dos boleto(s), por favor.**
please. *oon/dohs boh•leh•toh(s) pohr fah•bohr*

For today/tomorrow. **Para hoy/mañana.** *pah•rah oy/mah•nyah•nah*

A...ticket. **Un boleto...** *oon boh•leh•toh...*

one-way	**sencillo** *sehn•see•yoh*
return trip	**redondo** *rreh•dohn•doh*
first class	**de primera clase** *deh pree•meh•rah klah•seh*
business class	**de clase ejecutiva** *deh klah•seh ehe•ku•ti•vah*
economy class	**clase turista** *klah•seh tuh•rees•tah*

How much? **¿Cuánto es?** *kwahn•toh ehs*

Is there a discount **¿Hacen descuento a...?**
for...? *ah•sehn dehs•kwehn•toh ah...*

children	**niños** *nee•nyohs*
students	**estudiantes** *ehs•too•deeyahn•tehs*
senior citizens	**personas de la tercera edad** *pehr•soh•nahs deh lah tehr•seh•rah eh•dahd*
tourists	**turistas** *too•ris•tahs*

The express bus/ **El camión/tren express, por favor**
express train, please. *Ehl kah•meeyon/trehn express por fah•vohr*

The local bus/train, **El camion/tren local, por favor**
please. *Ehl kah•meeyon/trehn lo•kahl por fah•vohr*

I have an e-ticket. **Tengo un boleto electrónico**
tehn•go oon boh•leh•toh electroh•nikoh

Can I buy...		
a ticket on the bus/train?	**¿Puedo comprar el boleto a bordo del camión/tren ?** *pweh·doh kohm·prahr ehl boh·leh·toh ah bohr·doh dehl kah·meeyohn/trehn*
the ticket before boarding?	**¿El boleto antes de abordar?** *Ehl boh·leh·toh ahn·tehs deh abohr·dahr?*
How long is this ticket valid?	**¿Por cuánto tiempo es válido el boleto?** *Pohr cuahn·to tyehm·poh ehs vah·lidoh ehl boh·leh·toh?*
Can I return on the same ticket?	**¿Puedo volver con el mismo boleto?** *Pueh·doh vol·vehr con ehl mees·moh boh·leh·toh?*
I'd like to... my reservation.	**Quiero....mi reservación** *kyeh·roh.... mee rreh·sehr·vah·ceeohn*
cancel	**cancelar** *cahn·ceh·lahr*
change	**cambiar** *cahm·bee·ahr*
confirm	**confirmar** *cohn·feer·mahr*

For Time, see page 169.

Plane

How much is a taxi to the airport?	**¿Cuánto es la dejada al aeropuerto?** *kwahn·toh ehs lah deh·jah·dah ahl ah·eh·roh·pwehr·toh*
To...Airport, please.	**Al aeropuerto de..., por favor.** *ahl ah·eh·roh·pwehr·toh deh...pohr fah·bohr*
My airline is...	**Mi aerolínea es...** *mee ah·eh·roh·lee·neh·ah ehs...*
My flight leaves at...	**Mi vuelo sale a la/las...** *mee bweh·loh sah·leh ah lah/lahs...*
I'm in a rush.	**Tengo prisa.** *tehn·goh pree·sah*
Can you take an alternate route?	**¿Puede tomar otra ruta?** *pweh·deh toh·mahr oh·trah rroo·tah*
Can you drive faster/slower?	**¿Puede ir más deprisa/despacio ?** *pweh·deh eer mahs deh·pree·sah/dehs·pah·seeyoh*

Gates
Puertas

YOU MAY HEAR...

¿En qué aerolínea viaja? | What airline
ehn keh ah•eh•roh•lee•neh•ah beeyah•khah | are you flying?
¿Nacional o internacional? | Domestic or
nah•seeyoh•nahl oh een•tehr•nah•seeyoh•nahl | International?
¿Qué terminal? *keh tehr•mee•nahl* | What terminal?

YOU MAY SEE...

LLEGADAS	arrivals
SALIDAS	departures
RECLAMO DE EQUIPAJE	baggage claim
SEGURIDAD	security
VUELOS NACIONALES	domestic flights
VUELOS INTERNACIONALES	international flights
MOSTRADOR DE DOCUMENTACIÓN	check-in
DOCUMENTACIÓN CON BOLETO ELECTRÓNICO	e-ticket check-in
SALAS DE ABORDAR	departure gates

Checking In

Where's check-in?	**¿Dónde está el mostrador de documentación?**
	dohn·deh ehs·tah ehlmohs·trah·dohr deh
	doh·koo·mehn·tah·seeyohn
My name is...	**Me llamo...** *meh yah·moh...*
I'm going to...	**Voy a...** *boy ah...*
I have...	**Tengo...** *Tehn·goh*
one suitcase	**una maleta** *unah mah·leh·tah*
two suitcases	**dos maletas** *dohs mah·leh·tahs*
one piece	**una pieza** *unah pyeh·sah*
How much luggage is allowed?	**¿Cuánto equipaje está permitido?**
	kwahn·toh eh·kee·pah·kheh ehs·tah pehr·mee·tee·doh
Is that pounds or kilos?	**¿en libras o en kilos?** *Ehn lee·brahs o ehn kee·los*
Which terminal?	**¿Qué terminal?**
Which gate?	*¿Qué sala de abordar?*
I'd like a window/ an aisle seat.	**Quiero un asiento en ventana/pasillo.** *keeyeh·roh*
	oon ah·seeyehn·toh ehnbehn·tah·nah/pah·see·yoh
When do we leave/ arrive?	**¿A qué hora salimos/llegamos?**
	ah keh oh·rah sah·lee·mohs/yeh·gah·mohs
Is the flight delayed?	**¿Tiene retraso el vuelo?**
	teeyeh·nehrreh·trah·soh ehl bweh·loh
How late?	**¿Cuánto retraso tiene?**
	kwahn·toh rreh·trah·soh teeyeh·neh

Luggage

Where is/are...?	**¿Dónde está/están...?**
	dohn·deh ehs·tah/ehs·tahn...
the luggage trolleys	**los carritos para equipaje**
	lohs kah·rree·tohs pah·rah eh·kee·pah·kheh
the luggage lockers	**los casilleros para equipaje**
	lohs kah·see·yeh·rohs pah·rah eh·kee·pah·kheh

YOU MAY HEAR...

¡Siguiente! *see·geeyehn·teh*   Next!

Su pasaporte/boleto, por favor.   Your ticket/passport,
soo pah·sah·pohr·teh/boh·leh·toh pohr fah·bohr   please.

¿Va a documentar el equipaje?   Are you checking any
bah ah doh·koo·mehn·tahr ehl eh·kee·pah·kheh   luggage?

Eso es demasiado grande para equipaje   That's too large for a
de mano. *eh·soh ehs deh·mah·seeyah·*   carry-on [piece of hand
dohgrahn·deh pah·rah eh·kee·pah·kheh   luggage].
deh mah·noh

¿Hizo usted las maletas?   Did you pack these bags
ee·soh oos·ted lahs mah·leh·tahs   yourself?

¿Le entregó alguien algún paquete?   Did anyone give you
leh ehn·treh·goh ahl·geeyehn ahl·goon pah·keh·teh anything to carry?

Quítese los zapatos. *kee·teh·seh lohs sah·pah·tohs* Take off your shoes.

El vuelo...está abordando.
ehl bweh·loh...ehs·tah ah·bohr·dahn·doh   Now boarding...

---

the baggage claim   **el reclamo de equipaje**
                    ehl rreh·klah·moh deh eh·kee·pah·kheh

My luggage has   **Perdí/Me robaron mi equipaje.**
been lost/stolen.   *Pehr·dee meh roh·bah·rohn mee eh·kee·pah·kheh*

My suitcase is   **Mi maleta está dañada.**
damaged.   *mee mah·leh·tah ehs·tah dah·nyah·dah*

Finding your Way

Where is/are...?   **¿Dónde está/están...?** *dohn·deh ehs·tah/ehs·tahn...*

the currency   **la casa de cambio**
exchange   *lah kah·sah deh kahm·beeyoh*

the car hire	**la renta de autos** *lah rrehn·tah deh aw·tohs*
the exit	**la salida** *lah sah·lee·dah*
the taxis	**los taxis** *lohs tah·xees*
Is there…into town?	**¿Hay…que vaya a la ciudad?**
	aye…keh bah·yah ah lah seew·dahd
a bus	**un camión** *oon kah·meeyohn*
a train	**un tren** *oon trehn*
a Metro	**un metro** *oon meh·troh*

For Asking Directions, see page 33.

Train

Where's the train station?	**¿Dónde está la estación del tren?** *dohn·deh ehs·tah lah ehs·tah·seeyohn dehl trehn*
How far is it?	**¿A qué distancia está?** *ah kehdees·tahn·seeyah ehs·tah*
Where is/are…?	**¿Dónde está/están…?** *dohn·deh ehs·tah/ehs·tahn…*
the ticket office	**la taquilla** *lah tah·kee·yah*
the information desk	**los módulos de información** *lohs moh·doo·lohs deh een·fohr·mah·seeyohn*
the luggage lockers	**los casilleros** *lohs kah·see·yeh·rohs*
the platforms	**los andenes** *lohs ahn·deh·nehs*
Can I have a schedule [timetable]?	**¿Podría darme un itinerario?** *poh·dree·ah dahr·meh oon ee·tee·neh·rah·reeyoh*
How long is the trip?	**¿Cuánto dura el viaje?** *kwahn·toh doo·rah ehl beeyah·kheh*
Is it a direct train?	**¿Es un tren directo?** *Ehs uhn trehn dee·rehk·toh*
Do I have to change trains?	**¿Tengo que transbordar?** *tehn·goh keh trahnz·bohr·darh*
Is the train on time?	**¿Llega a tiempo el tren?** *yeh·gah ah tyehm·poh ehl trehn*

YOU MAY SEE...

ANDENES	platforms
INFORMACIÓN	information
RESERVACIONES	reservations
SALA DE ESPERA	waiting room
LLEGADAS	arrivals
SALIDAS	departures

Mexico has very limited passenger rail service. Instead, a plethora of private intercity bus lines serve this nation. The **Chihuahua Pacific Express (Chepe)** is a notable exception, an engineering feat and a 630 km spectacular trip.

Departures

Which track [platform] to...?	**¿De qué andén sale el tren a...?** *deh keh ahn•dehn sah•leh ehl trehn ah...*
Is this the track [platform]/ train to...?	**¿Es éste el andén/tren a...?** *ehs ehs•teh ehl*
Where is track [platform]...?	**¿Dónde está el andén...?** *dohn•deh ehs•tah ehl ahn•dehn...*
Where do I change for...?	**¿Dónde tengo que transbordar para...?** *dohn•deh tehn•goh keh trahnz•bohr•darh*

On Board

Can I sit here/open the window?	**¿Puedo sentarme aquí/abrir la ventana?** *pweh•doh sehn•tahr•meh ah•kee/ah•breer lah vehn•tah•nah*
That's my seat.	**Ése es mi asiento.** *eh•seh ehs meeah•seeyehn•toh*
Here's my reservation.	**Ésta es mi reservación** *Ehs•tah ehs mee reh•sehrvah•ciohn*

YOU MAY HEAR...

Boletos, por favor.
boh·leh·tohs pohr fah·bohr

Tiene que transbordar en...
teeyeh·neh keh trahnz·bohr·dahr ehn...

Próxima parada: Chihuahua.
proh·xee·mah pah·rah·dah chee·wah·wah

Tickets, please.

You have to change at...

Next stop... Chihuahua.

Bus

Where's the bus station?	**¿Dónde está la estación de camiones?** *dohn·deh ehs·tah lah ehs·tah·seeyohn deh kah·meeyoh·nehs*
How far is it?	**¿A qué distancia está?** *ah kehdees·tahn·seeyah ehs·tah*
How do I get to...?	**¿Cómo llego a...?** *koh·moh yeh·goh ah...*
Is this the bus to...?	**¿Es éste el camión a...?** *ehs ehs·teh ehl kah·meeyohn ah...*
Can you tell me when to get off?	**¿Podría decirme cuándo me tengo que bajar?** *poh·dree·ah deh·seer·meh kwahn·doh meh tehn·goh keh bah·khahr*
Do I have to change buses?	**¿Tengo que transbordar?** *tehn·goh keh trahnz·bohr·dahr*
Stop here, please!	**¡Pare aquí, por favor!** *pah·reh ah·kee pohr fah·bohr*

YOU MAY SEE...

PARADA DE CAMIONES	bus stop
PEDIR PARADA	request stop
SUBIR/BAJAR	entrance/exit
MARQUE SU BOLETO	stamp your ticket

The bus service in Mexico is extensive. For local service within a town or city, you pay as you board the bus. The fare depends on the distance you travel. Buses are known by different names: **camión, micro, pesera.** The **camión** is the public bus. **Micro** and **pesera** are privately operated; the **micro** is larger than the **pesera,** but not as large as the **camión.**

Metro

Where's the metro station?	**¿Dónde está la estación del metro?** *dohn·deh ehs·tah lah ehs·tah·seeyohn dehl meh·troh*
A map, please.	**Un mapa, por favor.** *oon mah·pah pohr fah·bohr*
Which line for…?	**¿Qué línea tengo que tomar para…?** *keh lee·neh·ah tehn·goh keh toh·mahr pah·rah…*
Which direction?	**¿En qué dirección?** *Eehn keh dee·rehc·siohn?*
Do I have to transfer [change]?	**¿Tengo que transbordar?** *tehn·goh keh trahnz·bohr·dahr*
Is this the metro to…?	**¿Éste es el metro para…?** *ehs·teh ehs ehl meh·troh pah·rah…*
How many stops to…?	**¿Cuántas paradas hasta?** *Kuahn·tahs pah·rah·dahs ahs·tah…?*

| Where are we? | **¿Dónde estamos?** *dohn·deh ehs·tah·mohs* |

For Tickets, see page 19.

> ℹ The new **Metrobus** system works very well as it uses exclusive lanes and electronic tickets sold in vending machines. This bus system currently goes along the longest avenue in Mexico City and crosses the city north to south.

Boat & Ferry

When is the ferry to…?	**¿Cuándo sale el transbordador a…?** *kwahn·doh sah·leh ehl trahnz·bohr·dah·dohr ah…*
Can I take my car?	**¿Puedo llevar el coche?** *pweh·doh yeh·bahr ehl koh·cheh*
What time is the next sailing?	**¿A qué hora es la próxima navegación?** *Ah keh orah ehs lah pro·xee·mah nah·vehgah·siohn*
Can I book a seat/cabin?	**¿Puedo reservar asiento/cabina?** *Pue·hdoh reh·sehr·bahr asyentoh/cah·bee·nah*
How long is the crossing?	**¿Cuánto tiempo toma cruzar?** *Kuahn·toh tyehm·poh toh·mah cru·sahr*

BOTE SALVAVIDAS life boats
CHALECO SALVAVIDAS life jackets

Ferries are not usually used by locals for getting around as they are located mainly at tourist attractions. There are ferries traveling from **Cozumel Island** to **Playa del Carmen**, from **Isla Mujeres** to **Cancún** and from **Mazatlán** to **La Paz** in the Gulf of California.

Taxi

Where can I get a taxi?	**¿Dónde puedo tomar un taxi?**
	dohn•deh pweh•doh toh•mahr oon tah•xee
Can you send a taxi?	**¿Puede enviar un taxi?**
	Pweh•deh ehn•vyar oon tah•xee?
Do you have the number for a taxi?	**¿Tiene el número de algún sitio de taxi?**
	teeyeh•neh ehl noo•meh•roh deh ahl•goon see•tee•oh deh tah•xee
I'd like a taxi now/ for tomorrow at...	**Quiero un taxi ahora/para mañana a la(s)...**
	keeyeh•roh oon tah•xee ah•oh•rah/pah•rah mah•nyah•nah ah lah(s)...
	pah•seh porh mee ehn/ah lah(s)...
I'm going to...	**Voy...** *boy...*
this address	**a esta dirección** *ah ehs•tah dee•rehk•seeyohn*
the airport	**al aeropuerto** *ahl ah•eh•roh•pwehr•toh*
the train station	**a la estación del tren ah lah**
	ehs•tah•seeyohn dehl trehn
I'm late.	**Voy retrasado.** *vohee rreh•trah•sah•doh*

Can you drive faster/ slower?	**¿Puede ir más deprisa/despacio?**
	pweh•deh eer mahs deh•pree•sah dehs•pah•seeyoh
Stop/Wait here.	**Pare/Espere aquí.** *pah•reh/ehs•peh•reh ah•kee*
How much?	**¿Cuánto es?** *kwahn•toh ehs*
You said it would cost…	**Dijo que costaría…** *dee•khoh kehkohs•tah•ree•ah…*
Keep the change.	**Quédese con el cambio.** *keh•deh•seh kohn ehl kahm•beeyoh*

YOU MAY HEAR…

¿Para donde va? *pah•rah dohn•deh vah* Where to?

¿Cuál es la dirección? What's the address?
kwahl ehs lahdee•rehk•seeyohn

Hay un recargo nocturno al aeropuerto *Aee* There's a nighttime/
oon reh•cahr•go nok•tur•noh ahl ahero•pwehr•toh? airport surcharge.

In major Mexican cities, taxis are reasonably priced. When entering the taxi, make sure the meter is turned on; it should register a base fare. For safety, make sure you only hail a licensed taxi; these are white with a red horizontal strip at the side of the car. You can also call ahead to book a licensed taxi service.

In some Spanish-speaking countries **coger** means "to get" or "to catch", as in: **¿Dónde puedo coger un taxi?** (Where can I catch a taxi?) However, in Mexico, **coger** is a vulgarity meaning **"to have sex"**. Travelers to Mexico should always use **tomar** or **abordar** when they want to express the verb "to get" or "to catch" (**¿Dónde puedo tomar un taxi?).**

Bicycle & Motorbike

I'd like to hire…	**Quiero rentar…** *keeyeh·roh rrehn·tahr…*
a bicycle	**una bicicleta** *oo·nah bee·see·kleh·tah*
a moped	**una motoneta** *oo·nah moh·toh·neh·tah*
a motorcycle	**una motocicleta** *oo·nah moh·toh·see·kleh·tah*
How much per day/week?	**¿Cuánto cuesta por día/semana ?** *kwahn·toh kwehs·tah pohr dee·ah/seh·mah·nah*
Can I have a helmet/lock?	**¿Puede darme un casco/candado ?** *pweh·deh dahr·meh oon kahs·koh/kahn·dah·doh*
I have a puncture/ flat tyre.	**Se ponchó una llanta.** *se pon·tchoh unah jahn·tah*

Car Hire

Where's the car hire?	**¿Dónde puedo rentar un auto?** *dohn·deh pweh·doh rrehn·tahr oon aw·toh*
I'd like…	**Quiero…** *keeyeh·roh…*
a cheap/small car	**un auto barato/compacto** *oonaw·toh bah·rah·toh/kohm·pahk·toh*
an automatic/ a manual	**un auto automático/manual** *oon autto autto·mah·teeco/mahn·uahl*
air conditioning	**un auto con aire acondicionado** *oon aw·toh kohn ayee·reh ah·kohn·dee·seeyoh·nah·doh*

a car seat	**un asiento de niño**
	oon ah·seeyehn·toh deh nee·nyoh
How much...?	**¿Cuánto cobran...?** *kwahn·toh koh·brahn...*
per day/week	**por día/semana** *pohr dee·ah/seh·mah·nah*
per kilometer	**por kilómetro** *pohr kee·loh·meh·troh*
for unlimited	**por kilometraje ilimitado pohr**
mileage	*kee·loh·meh·trah·kheh ee·lee·mee·tah·doh*
with insurance	**con el seguro** *kohn ehl seh·goo·roh*
Are there any	**¿Ofrecen algún descuento?**
discounts?	*oh·freh·sehnahl·goon dehs·kwehn·toh*

YOU MAY HEAR...

¿Tiene licencia de conducir international?	Do you have an
teeyeh·neh lee·sehn·seeyah deh kohn·doo·seer	international driver's
een·tehr·nah·seeyoh·nahl	license?
Su pasaporte, por favor.	Your passport, please.
soo pah·sah·pohr·teh pohr fah·bohr	
¿Quiere seguro?	Do you want insurance?
keeyeh·reh seh·goo·roh	
Necesitaré un depósito.	I'll need a deposit.
neh·seh·see·tah·reh oon deh·poh·see·toh	
Ponga sus iniciales/Firme aquí.	Initial/Sign here.
Pohn·gah soos eenee·syah·lehs/Feer·meh ah·kee	

Fuel Station

Where's the fuel	**¿Dónde está la gasolinera?**
station?	*dohn·deh ehs·tah lah gah·soh·lee·neh·rah*
Fill it up.	**Lleno.** *yeh·noh*
...liters, please.	**...litros, por favor** *...lee·trohs por fah·bohr*

I'll pay in cash/by credit card.	**Voy a pagar en efectivo/con tarjeta de crédito.** *boy ah pah•gahr ehn eh•fehk•tee•boh/kohn tahr•kheh•tah deh kreh•dee•toh*

For Numbers, see page 167.

YOU MAY SEE...

GASOLINA	gas [petrol]
SIN PLOMO	unleaded
MAGNA SIN	regular
MAGNA PREMIUM	premium [super]
DIÉSEL	diesel

Asking Directions

Is this the way to...?	**¿Es ésta la ruta a...?** *ehs ehs•tah lah rroo•tah ah...*
How far is it to...?	**¿A qué distancia está...?** *ah kehdees•tahn•seeyah ehs•tah...*
Where's...?	**¿Dónde está...?** *dohn•deh ehs•tah...*
...Street	**la calle...** *lah kah•yeh...*
this address	**esta dirección** *ehs•tah dee•rehk•seeyohn*

YOU MAY HEAR...

Derecho/recto *deh·reh·choh/rrehk·toh* — straight ahead
a la izquierda *ah lah ees·keeyehr·dah* — left
a la derecha *ah lah deh·reh·chah* — right
en/doblando la esquinaehn/ *doh·blahn·doh lah ehs·kee·nah* — around the corner
frente a *frehn·teh ah* — opposite
detrás de *deh·trahs deh* — behind
al lado de *ahl lah·doh deh* — next to
después de *dehs·pwehs deh* — after
al norte/sur *ahl nohr·teh/soor* — north/south
al este/oeste *ahl ehs·teh/oh·ehs·teh* — east/west
en el semáforo *en ehl seh·mah·foh·roh* — at the traffic light
en el cruce en *ehl kroo·seh* — at the intersection

the highway [motorway] — **la autopista** *lah aw·toh·pees·tah*
Can you show me on the map? — **¿Me lo puede indicar en el mapa?** *meh loh pweh·deh een·dee·kahr ehn ehl mah·pah*
I'm lost. — **Me perdí.** *meh pehr·dee*

Parking

Can I park here?	**¿Puedo estacionarme aquí?**
	pweh·doh es·tah·seeyoh·nahr·meh ah·kee
Where's...?	**¿Dónde está...?** *Dohn·de ehs·tah...?*
the parking garage	**el garaje de estacionamiento**
	ehl ga·ra·heh deh estah·syo·nah·myehn·toh
the parking lot [car park]	**el lote de estacionamiento**
	ehl lo·teh deh estah·syonah·myehn·toh
the parking attendant	**el encargado del estacionamiento**
	ehl ehn·kahr·gah·doh del estah·syonah·myehn·toh
How much...?	**¿Cuánto cobran...?** *kwahn·toh koh·brahn...*
per hour	**por hora** *pohr oh·rah*
per day	**por día** *pohr dee·ah*
for overnight	**por la noche** *pohr lah noh·cheh*

Parking is permitted on most streets. Some areas offer restricted parking with parking meters. In zones where parking is not allowed you may see **PROHIBIDO ESTACIONARSE** (no parking) or sometimes you will find a yellow line on the curb. Traffic authorities may tow your vehicle for illegal parking and payment of fines (with a credit or debit card) on the spot may be required.

Breakdown & Repair

My car broke down/ won't start.	**El auto se descompuso/no arranca.**
	ehl aw·toh seh des·kohm·poo·soh/nohah·rrahn·kah
Can you fix it (today)?	**¿Puede arreglarlo (hoy mismo)?**
	pweh·deh ah·rreh·glahr·loh (oy meez·moh)
When will it be ready?	**¿Cuándo estará listo?**
	kwahn·doh ehs·tah·rah lees·toh
How much?	**¿Cuánto es?** *kwahn·toh ehs*

YOU MAY SEE...

 ALTO — stop

 CEDA EL PASO — yield [give way]

 PROHIBIDO ESTACIONARSE — no parking

 UN SOLO SENTIDO — one way

 NO ENTRAR — no entry

 NO SE PERMITEN VEHICULOS — no vehicles allowed

 PROHIBIDO REBASAR — no passing

 SEÑAL DE TRÁFICO ADELANTE — traffic lights ahead

 SALIDA — exit

Accidents

There was an accident. **Hubo un accidente.** *oo·boh oon ahk·see·dehn·teh*

Call an ambulance/ the police. **Llame a una ambulancia/la policía.** *yah·meh ah oo·nah ahm·boo·lahn·seeyah/lah poh·lee·see·ah*

Places to Stay

ESSENTIAL

Can you recommend a hotel?	**¿Puede recomendarme un hotel?** *pweh•deh rreh•koh•mehn•dahr•meh oon oh•tehl*
I made a reservation.	**Tengo una reserva.** *tehn•goh oo•nah rreh•sehr•bah*
My name is…	**Me llamo…** *meh yah•moh…*
Do you have a room…?	**¿Tienen habitaciones…?** *teeyeh•nehnah•bee•tah•seeyoh•nehs…*
for one/two	**sencillas/dobles** *sehn•see•yahs/doh•blehs*
with a bathroom	**con baño** *kohn bah•nyoh*
with air conditioning	**con aire acondicionado** *kohn ayee•reh ah•kohn•dee•seeyoh•nah•doh*
For…	**Para…** *pah•rah…*
tonight	**esta noche** *ehs•tah noh•cheh*
two nights	**dos noches** *dohs noh•chehs*
one week	**una semana** *oo•nah seh•mah•nah*
How much?	**¿Cuánto es?** *kwahn•toh ehs*
Is there anything cheaper?	**¿Hay alguna tarifa más barata?** *aye ahl•goo•nah tah•ree•fah mahs bah•rah•tah*
When's checkout?	**¿A qué hora hay que desocupar la habitación?** *ah keh oh•rah aye keh deh•soh•koo•pahr lah ah•bee•tah•seeyohn*
Can I leave this in the safe?	**¿Puedo dejar esto en la caja fuerte?** *pweh•doh deh•khahr ehs•toh ehn lah kah•khah fwehr•teh*
Can I leave my bags?	**¿Podría dejar mi equipaje?** *poh•dree•ah deh• khahr mee eh•kee•pah•kheh*

| Can I have the bill/ a receipt? | ¿Me da la factura/un comprobante? *meh dah lah fahk·too·rah/oon kohm·proh·bahn·teh* |
| I'll pay in cash/ by credit card. | **Voy a pagar en efectivo/con tarjeta de crédito.** *boy ah pah·gahr ehn eh·fehk·tee·boh/kohn tahr·kheh·tah deh kreh·dee·toh* |

There are a variety of places to stay in Mexico. Hotels are rated from one to five stars, with five stars being the most expensive and having the most amenities. Other unique accommodations in Mexico include spas, resorts, hostels and lodges.

Somewhere to Stay

Can you recommend...?	¿Puede recomendarme ...? *pweh·deh rreh·koh·mehn·dahr·meh...*
a hotel	**un hotel** *oon oh·tehl*
a hostel	**un albergue** *oon ahl·behr·gheh*
a campsite	**un campamento** *oon kahm·pah·mehn·toh*
a bed and breakfast (B&B)	**una posada** *oonah poh·sah·dah*
What is it near?	¿Qué hay cerca? *keh aye sehr·kah*
How do I get there?	¿Cómo llego? *koh·moh yeh·goh*

If you didn't reserve accommodations before your trip, visit the local **Oficina de Turismo** (Tourist Information Office) or any local travel agency for recommendations on places to stay.

At the Hotel

I have a reservation.	**Tengo una reservación.**
	tehn·goh oo·nah rreh·sehr·bah·seeyohn
My name is…	**Me llamo…** *meh yah·moh…*
Do you have a room…?	**¿Tiene una habitación…?**
	teeyeh·neh oo·nah ah·bee·tah·seeyohn…
with a toilet/ shower	**con baño/ regadera**
	kohn oon bah·nyoh/oo·nah rreh·gah·deh·rah
with air conditioning	**con aire acondicionado**
	kohn ayee·reh ah·kohn·dee·seeyoh·nah·doh
that's smoking/ non-smoking	**para fumadores/no fumadores**
	pah·rah foo·mah·doh·rehs /noh foo·mah·doh·rehs
For…	**Para…** *pah·rah…*
tonight	**esta noche** *ehs·tah noh·cheh*
two nights	**dos noches** *dohs noh·chehs*
a week	**una semana** *oo·nah seh·mah·nah*
Do you have…?	**¿El hotel tiene…?**
	ehl oh·tehl teeyeh·neh…
a computer	**una computadora**
	oo·nah kohm·poo·tah·doh·rah
an elevator [a lift]	**un elevador** *oon eh·leh·bah·dohr*

(wireless) internet service	**acceso (inalámbrico) a Internet** *ahk•seh•soh (een•ah•lahm•bree•koh) ah een•tehr•neht*
room service	**servicio a la habitación** *sehr•bee•seeyoh ah lah ah•bee•tah•seeyohn*
a pool	**una alberca** *oo•nah ahl•behr•kah*
a gym	**un gimnasio** *oon kheem•nah•seeyoh*
I need…	**Necesito…** *neh•seh•see•toh…*
an extra bed	**otra cama** *oh•trah kah•mah*
a cot	**un catre** *oon kah•treh*
a crib	**una cuna** *oo•nah koo•nah*

YOU MAY HEAR…

Su pasaporte/tarjeta de crédito, por favor. *soo pah•sah•pohr•teh/tahr•kheh•tah deh kreh•dee•toh pohr fah•bohr*	Your passport/ credit card, please.
Llene este formulario. *yeh•neh ehs•teh fohr•moo•lah•reeyoh*	Fill out this form.
Firme aquí. *feer•meh ah•kee*	Sign here.

Price

How much per night/week?	**¿Cuánto cuesta por noche/semana?** *kwahn•toh kwehs•tah pohr noh•cheh/seh•mah•nah*
Does that include breakfast/tax?	**¿El precio incluye el desayuno/IVA?** *ehl preh•seeyoh een•kloo•yeh ehldeh•sah•yoo•noh/ ee•bah*
Are there any discounts?	**¿Hay algún descuento?** *Ah•ee algoon dehs•kwen•toh*

Preferences

Can I see the room?	**¿Puedo ver la habitación?**
	pweh·doh behr lah ah·bee·tah·seeyohn
I'd like a…room.	**Quisiera una habitación**
	kee·see·yeh·rah oo·nah abee·tah·syon
better	**mejor** *meh·hor*
bigger	**más grande**
	mahs grahn·deh
cheaper	**más barata**
	mahs bah·rah·tah
quieter	**más tranquila**
	mahs trahn·kee·lah
I'll take it.	**La tomo.** *Lah toh·moh*
No, I won't take it.	**No la tomo** *No lah toh·moh*

YOU MAY SEE…

EMPUJAR/JALAR	push/pull
BAÑO/SANITARIOS	bathroom [toilet]
REGADERA	shower
ELEVADOR	elevator [lift]
ESCALERAS	stairs
MÁQUINAS DISPENSADORAS	vending machines
HIELO	ice
LAVANDERÍA	laundry
NO MOLESTAR	do not disturb
PUERTA DE INCENDIOS	fire door
SALIDA (DE EMERGENCIA)	(emergency) exit
SERVICIO DE DESPERTADOR	wake-up call

Questions

Where is/are…?	**¿Dónde está…?**
	dohn•deh ehs•tah…
the bar	**el bar** *ehl bahr*
the bathroom	**el baño** *ehl bah•nyoh*
the elevator [lift]	**el elevador** *ehl eh•leh•bah•dohr*
Can I have…?	**¿Puede darme…?**
	pweh•deh dahr•meh…
a blanket	**una cobija** *oo•nah coh•bee•khah*
an iron	**una plancha** *oo•nah plahn•chah*
the room key/	**la llave/tarjeta de la habitación**
key card	*ah yah•beh/tar•kheh•tah deh lah ah•bee•ta•seeyon*
a pillow	**una almohada** *oo•nah ahl•moh•ah•dah*
soap	**jabón** *khah•bohn*
toilet paper	**papel higiénico** *pah•pehlee•kheeyeh•nee•koh*
a towel	**una toalla** *oo•nah toh•ah•yah*
Do you have an adapter for this?	**¿Tiene un adaptador para esto?** *teeyeh•neh oon ah•dahp•tah•dohr pah•rah ehs•toh*
How do you turn on the lights?	**¿Cómo prendo las luces?** *koh•moh prehn•doh lahs loo•sehs*
Can you wake me at…?	**¿Podría despertarme a las…?** *poh•dree•ah dehs•pehr•tahr•meh ah lah/lahs…*
Can I leave this in the safe?	**¿Puedo dejar esto en la caja fuerte?** *pweh•doh deh•khahr ehs•toh ehn lahkah•khah fwehr•teh*
Can I have my things from the safe?	**¿Podría darme mis cosas de la caja fuerte?** *poh•dree•ah dahr•meh mees koh•sahs deh lah kah•khah fwehr•teh*
Is there mail /a message for me?	**¿Hay correo/algún mensaje para mí?** *aye koh•rreh•oh/ahl•goon mehn•sah•kheh pah•rah mee*
Do you have a laundry service?	**¿Tienen servicio de lavandería?** *Tyeh•nehn sehr•bee•cyo deh lah•vahn•deh•ree•ah*

Problems

There's a problem.	**Hay un problema.** *aye oon proh·bleh·mah*
I lost my key/key card.	**Perdí la llave/tarjeta electrónica.** *pehr·dee lah yah·beh/tahr·kheh·tah eh·lehk·troh·nee·kah*
I've locked my key/ key card in the room.	**Dejé mi llave/tarjeta dentro de la habitación** *Deh·kheh mee jah·beh/tar·kheh·tah dehn·troh deh lah ah·bee·tah·seeyohn*
There's no hot water/toilet paper.	**No hay agua caliente/papel higiénico.** *no aye ah·gwah kah·leeyehn·teh/pah·pehl ee·kheeyeh·nee·koh*
The room is dirty.	**La habitación está sucia.** *lah ah·bee·tah· seeyohn ehs·tah soo·seeyah*
There are bugs in the room.	**Hay insectos en la habitación.** *aye een·sehk·tohs ehn lah ah·bee·tah·seeyohn*
the air conditioning	**el aire acondicionado** *ehl ayee·reh ah·kohn·dee·seeyoh·nah·doh*
the fan	**el ventilador** *ehl behn·tee·lah·dohr*
the heat [heating]	**la calefacción** *lah kah·leh·fahk·seeyohn*
the light	**la luz** *lah loos*
the TV	**la televisión** *lah teh·leh·bee·seeyohn*
the toilet	**el excusado** *ehl ehx·koo·sah·doh*
...doesn't work.	**...no funciona** *...noh foon·syo·nah*
Can you fix...?	**¿Pueden arreglar...?** *pweh·dehn ah·rreh·glahr...*
I'd like another room.	**Quiero otra habitación.** *keeyeh·roh oh·trah ah·bee·tah·seeyohn*

Voltage in Mexico for electrical appliances is **110 volts, 60 Hz.** A converter and/or an adapter may be needed for foreign appliances.

Checking Out

When's check-out?	**¿A qué hora hay que desocupar la habitación?** *ah keh oh•rah aye keh deh•soh•koo•pahr lah ah•bee•tah•seeyohn*
Can I leave my bags here until…?	**¿Puedo dejar mis maletas aquí hasta…?** *pweh•doh deh•khahr mees mah•leh•tahs ah•kee ahs•tah…*
Can I have an itemized bill/ a receipt?	**¿Puede darme una factura desglosada/un comprobante?** *pweh•deh dahr•meh oo•nahfahk•too•rah dehs•gloh•sah•dah/oon kohm•proh•bahn•teh*
I think there's a mistake.	**Creo que hay un error.** *kreh•oh keh aye oon eh•rrohr*
I'll pay in cash/by credit card.	**Voy a pagar en efectivo/con tarjeta de crédito.** *boy ah pah•gahr ehn eh•fehk•tee•boh/kohn tahr•kheh•tah deh kreh•dee•toh*

When asking for a public restroom, say **¿Dónde está el baño?** or **¿Dónde están los sanitarios?** Most speakers of Mexican Spanish will use **baño**, but **sanitarios** will be used on signs. **Tipping** the porter in hotels is customary in Mexico. The amount varies based on the type of hotel. The more exclusive the hotel, the larger the tip should be.

Renting

I reserved an apartment/a room.	**Reservé un departamento/una habitación.** *rreh·sehr·beh oon deh·pahr·tah·mehn·toh/oo·nah ah·bee·tah·seeyohn*
My name is…	**Me llamo…** *meh yah·moh…*
Can I have the key/ key card?	**¿Puede darme la llave/tarjeta electrónica?** *pweh·deh dahr·meh lah / tahr·kheh·tah*
Are there…?	**¿Hay…?** *aye…*
dishes	**platos** *plah·tohs*
pillows	**almohadas** *ahl·moh·ah·dahs*
sheets	**sábanas** *sah·bah·nahs*
towels	**toallas** *toh·ah·yahs*
kitchen utensils	**cubiertos** *koo·beeyehr·tohs*
When do I put out the bins /recycling?	**¿Dónde coloco los botes/reciclaje?** *Dohn·deh koh·loh·coh los boh·tehs/reh·si·clah·heh?*
…is broken.	**…está descompuesto.** *Ehs·tah dehs·com·pwes·toh*
How does…work?	**¿Cómo funciona…?** *koh·moh foon·seeyoh·nah…*
the air conditioner	**el aire acondicionado** *ehl ayee·rehah·kohn·dee·seeyoh·nah·doh*
the dishwasher	**el lavaplatos** *ehl lah·vah·plah·tohs*
the freezer	**el congelador** *ehl kohn·kheh·lah·dohr*
the heater	**la calefacción** *lah kah·leh·fahk·seeyohn*
the microwave	**el microondas** *ehl mee·kroh·ohn·dahs*
the refrigerator	**el refrigerador** *ehl rreh·free·kheh·rah·dohr*
the stove	**la estufa** *lah ehs·too·fah*
the washing machine	**la lavadora** *lah lah·bah·doh·rah*

Domestic Items

I need…	**Necesito…** *neh·seh·see·toh…*
an adapter	**un adaptador** *oon ah·dahp·tah·dohr*

aluminum foil	**papel aluminio** *pah·pehl ah·loo·mee·neeyoh*
a bottle opener	**un destapador** *oon dehs·tah·pah·dohr*
a broom	**una escoba** *oo·nah ehs·koh·bah*
a can opener	**un abrelatas** *oon ah·breh·lah·tahs*
cleaning supplies	**productos de limpieza**
	proh·dook·tohs deh leem·peeyeh·sah
a corkscrew	**un sacacorchos** *oon sah·kah·kohr·chohs*
detergent	**detergente** *deh·tehr·khehn·teh*
dishwashing liquid	**líquido lavaplatos** *lee·kee·doh lah·bah·plah·toh*
bin bags	**bolsas de basura** *bohl·sahs dehbah·soo·rah*
a lightbulb	**un foco** *oon foh·koh*
matches	**cerillos** *seh·ree·yohs*
a mop	**un trapeador** *oon trah·peh·ah·dohr*
napkins	**servilletas** *sehr·bee·yeh·tahs*
paper towels	**toallas de papel** *toh·ah·yahs deh pah·pehl*
plastic wrap	**plástico transparente**
[cling film]	*plahs·tee·kohtrahns·pah·rehn·teh*
a plunger	**un destapacaños** *oon desh·tah·pah·kahn·yeeohs·*
scissors	**tijeras** *tee·kheh·rahs*
a vacuum cleaner	**una aspiradora** *oo·nah ahs·pee·rah·doh·rah*

At the Hostel

Is there a bed available?	**¿Hay camas disponibles?** *ahy kah·mahs dees·poh·nee·blehs*
I'd like…	**¿Me puede dar…?** *meh pweh·deh dahr…*
a single/double room	**una habitación sencilla/doble** *oo·nah ah·bee·tah·seeyohn sehn·see·yah/doh·bleh*
a blanket	**una cobija** *oo·nah koh·bee·khah*
a pillow	**una almohada** *oo·nah ahl·moh·ah·dah*
sheets	**sábanas** *sah·bah·nahs*
a towel	**una toalla** *oo·nah toh·ah·yah*
Do you have lockers?	**¿Tiene casilleros?** *Ty·eh·neh cah·see·jeh·rohs?*

When do you lock up?	**¿A qué hora cierran las puertas?**
	ah keh oh•rah seeyeh•rrahn lahs pwehr•tahs
Do I need a membership card?	**¿Necesito una tarjeta de socio?**
	neh•seh•see•toh oo•nah tahr•kheh•tah de soh•seeyoh
Here's my international student card.	**Aquí tiene mi credencial internacional de estudiante.** *ah•kee teeyeh•neh mee kreh•dehn•seeahl een•tehr•nah•seeyoh•nahl deh ehs•too•deeyahn•teh*

Going Camping

Can I camp here?	**¿Puedo acampar aquí?** *pweh•doh ah•kahm•pahr ah•kee*
Where's the campsite?	**¿Dónde está el campamento?**
	dohn•deh ehs•tah ehl kahm•pah•mehn•toh
What is the charge per day/week?	**¿Cuánto cobran por día/semana?**
	kwahn•toh koh•brahn pohr dee•ah/seh•mah•nah
Are there...?	**¿Hay...?** *aye...*
cooking facilities	**instalaciones para cocinar**
	eens•tah•lah•seeyoh•nehs pah•rah koh•see•nahr
electric outlets	**enchufes eléctricos** *ehn•choo•fehs eh•lehk•tree•kohs*
laundry facilities	**servicio de lavandería**
	sehr•bee•seeyoh deh lah•bahn•deh•ree•ah
showers	**regaderas** *rreh•gah•deh•rahs*
tents for hire	**renta de tiendas de campaña**
	rrehn•tah deh teeyehn•dahs deh kahm•pah•nya
Where can I empty the chemical toilet?	**¿Dónde puedo vaciar el excusadoquímico?** *dohn•deh pweh•doh bah•seeyahr ehl ehx•koo•sah•doh kee•mee•koh*

YOU MAY SEE...

| **AGUA POTABLE** | drinking water |
| **PROHIBIDO HACER PARRILLADAS/HOGUERAS** | no fires/barbecues |

Communications

Where's an internet cafe?	**¿Dónde hay un café Internet?** *dohn·deh aye oon cah·feh een·tehr·neht*
Can I access the internet/check email?	**¿Puedo entrar a Internet/revisar el correo electrónico?** *pweh·doh ehn·trahrah een·tehr·neht/reh·bee·sahr ehl koh·rreh·oh eh·lehk·troh·nee·koh*
How much per (half) hour?	**¿Cuánto cuesta por (media) hora?** *kwan·toh kwehs·tah pohr (meh·deeyah) oh·rah*
How do I connect/ log on?	**¿Cómo me conecto/inicio la sesión?** *koh·moh meh koh·nehk·toh/ee·nee·seeyoh lah seh·seeyohn*
A phone card, please.	**Una tarjeta de teléfono, por favor.** *oo·nah tahr·kheh·tah deh teh·leh·foh·noh pohr fah·bohr*
Can I have your phone number?	**¿Me puede dar su número de teléfono?** *meh pweh·deh dahr soo noo·meh·roh deh teh·leh·foh·noh*
Here's my number /e-mail.	**Este es mi número/Esta es mi dirección de correo electrónico.** *ehs·teh ehs mee noo·meh·roh/ ehs·tah ehs mee dee·rehk·seeyohn deh koh·rreh·oh eh·lehk·troh·nee·koh*
Call me.	**Llámeme.** *yah·meh·meh*
E-mail me.	**Envíeme un correo electrónico.** *ehn·bee·eh·meh oon koh·rreh·oh eh·lehk·troh·nee·koh*
Hello. This is…	**Hola. Soy…** *oh·lah soy…*
Can I speak to…?	**¿Puedo hablar con…?** *pweh·doh ah·blahr kohn…*
Can you repeat that?	**¿Puede repetir eso?** *pweh·deh rreh·peh·teer eh·soh*
I'll call back later.	**Llamaré más tarde.** *yah·mah·reh mahs tahr·deh*
Bye.	**Adiós.** *ah·deeyohs*
Where's the post office?	**¿Dónde está la oficina de correos?** *dohn·deh ehs·tah lah oh·fee·see·nah deh koh·rreh·ohs*
I'd like to send this to…	**Quiero mandar esto a…** *keeyeh·roh mahn·dahr ehs·toh ah…*

There are many **internet cafes** throughout Mexico, especially in bigger cities. These are very popular, as not everyone has personal access to the internet. You usually pay a set fee per hour.

Online

Where's an internet cafe?	**¿Dónde hay un café Internet?**
	dohn•deh aye oon cah•feh een•tehr•neht
Does it have wireless internet?	**¿Tiene Internet inalámbrico?**
	teeyeh•neh een•tehr•neht een•ah•lahm•bree•koh
What is the WiFi password?	**¿Cuál es la contraseña del WiFi?** *Kwahl ehs lah*
	kohn•trah•seh•nyah dehl wee-fee?
Is the WiFi free?	**¿Es gratis el WiFi?** *Ehs grah•tees el Wee-Fee?*
Do you have bluetooth?	**¿Tienen Bluetooth?** *Tyeh•nehn Bluetooth*
Can you show me how to turn on/off the computer?	**¿Me muestra cómo encender/apagar la computadora?** *Meh mwes•trah koh•mo ehn sehn•dehr lah kom•poo•tah•doh•rah?*
Can I…?	**¿Puedo…?** *pweh•doh…*
access the internet	**entrar a Internet** *ehn•trahr ah een•tehr•neht*
check my e-mail	**revisar el correo electrónico**
	rreh•bee•sahr ehl koh•rreh•oh eh•lehk•troh•nee•koh
print	**imprimir** *eem•pree•meer*
plug in/charge my laptop/iPhone/iPad/BlackBerry?	**Conectar/recargar mi laptop/iPhone/iPad/BlackBerry?** *Coh•neck•tahr/Reh•car•gahr mee laptop/iPhone/iPad/Blackberry*
access Skype?	**Acceder a Skype** *ahk•seh•dehr ah Skype*
How much per half hour/hour?	**¿Cuánto cuesta por (media) hora?**
	kwahn•toh kwehs•tah pohr (meh•deeyah) oh•rah
How do I…?	**¿Cómo…?** *koh•moh…*

connect/disconnect	**me conecto/desconecto**
	meh koh·nehk·toh/dehs·koh·nehk·toh
log on/off	**inicio/cierro la sesión**
	ee·nee·seeyoh/seeyeh·rroh lah seh·seeyohn
type this symbol	**escribo este símbolo**
	ehs·kree·boh ehs·teh seem·boh·loh
What's your e-mail?	**¿Cuál es su dirección de correo electrónico?**
	kwahl ehs soo dee·rehk·seeyohn deh koh·rreh·oh
	eh·lehk·troh·nee·koh
My e-mail is…	**Mi dirección de correo electrónico es…**
	mee dee·rehk·seeyohn deh koh·rreh·oh
	eh·lehk·troh·nee·koh ehs…

Do you have a scanner? **¿Tiene un escáner?** *Tye·neh oon es·kah·nehr?*

Social Media

Are you on Facebook/Twitter?	**¿Estás en Facebook/Twitter?**
	Ehs·tahs ehn Facebook/Twitter?
What's your user name?	**¿Cuál es tu nombre de usuario?**
	Kwahl ehs too nohm·breh deh u·swah·ryoh?
I'll add you as a friend.	**Te añadiré como amigo.**
	Teh a·nyah·dee·reh co·moh amee·go
I'll follow you on Twitter.	**Te seguiré en Twitter.** *Te seh·guee·reh ehn Twitter*
Are you following…?	**¿Estás siguiendo a…?** *ehs·tahs see·ghee·ehn·do ah*
I'll put the pictures on Facebook/Twitter.	**Pondré las fotos en Facebook/Twitter**
	Pond·reh lahs foh·tohs ehn Facebook/Twittter
I'll tag you in the pictures.	**Te etiquetaré en las fotos.**
	Teh ehti·ketah·reh ehn lahs foh·tohs

Phone

| A phone card/prepaid phone, please. | **Una tarjeta de teléfono/Un teléfono prepago, por favor.** *oo·nah tahr·kheh·tah deh teh·leh·foh·noh/ oon teh·leh·foh·noh preh·pah·goh pohr fah·bohr* |

YOU MAY SEE...

CERRAR	close
BORRAR	delete
CORREO ELECTRÓNICO	email
SALIR	exit
AYUDA	help
MENSAJERO INSTANTÁNEO	instant messenger
INTERNET	internet
INICIAR SESIÓN	log in
NUEVO (MENSAJE)	new (message)
PRENDER/APAGAR	on/off
ABRIR	open
IMPRIMIR	print
GUARDAR	save
ENVIAR	send
NOMBRE DE USUARIO/CONTRASEÑA	username/password
INTERNET INALÁMBRICO	wireless internet

How much?	**¿Cuánto es?** kwahn·toh ehs
Where's the pay phone?	**¿Dónde está el teléfono público?** dohn·deh ehs·tah ehl teh·leh·foh·noh pooh·blee·koh
What's the area country code for...?	**¿Cuál es el código local/código de país para...?** kwahl ehs ehl koh·dee·goh loh·kahl/koh·dee·goh deh pah·ees pah·rah...
What's the number for Information?	**¿Cuál es el número de información?** kwahl ehs ehl noo·meh·roh deh een·fohr·mah·seeyohn
I'd like the number for...	**Necesito el número de teléfono de...** neh·seh·see·toh ehl noo·meh·roh deh teh·leh·foh·noh deh...
I'd like to call collect [reverse the charges].	**Quiero llamar por cobrar** kye·roh yah·mahr por koh·brahr

My phone doesn't work here.	**Mi teléfono no funciona aquí**
	Mee teh•leh•foh•noh no fun•cyo•nah a•kee
What network are you on?	**¿A qué red pertenecen?**
	Ah keh rehd pehr•teh•neh•sehn
Is it 3G?	**¿Es 3G?** *Ehs 3G*
I have run out of credit/minutes.	**Ya no tengo crédito/minutos**
	yah no tehn•goh creh•dee•toh/mee•noo-tohs
Can I buy some credit?	**¿Puedo comprar crédito?**
	Pweh-doh cohm•prahr creh-dee-toh
Do you have a phone charger?	**¿Tiene un cargador de teléfono?**
	Tyeh•neh oon cahr•gah•dohr deh teh•leh•foh•noh
Can I have your number?	**¿Me puede dar su número de teléfono?** *meh*
	pweh•deh dahr soo noo•meh•roh deh teh•leh•foh•noh
Here's my number.	**Este es mi número.** *ehs•teh ehs mee noo•meh•roh*
Please call/text me.	**Llámeme, por favor.** *yah•meh•meh pohr fah•bohr/*
	Envíeme un mensaje de texto, por favor.
	ehn•beeyeh•meh oon mehn•sah•kheh deh tehx•toh pohr
	fah•bohr
I'll call/text you.	**Te llamo/envió un texto**
	teh yah•moh/en•vee•oh oon tehx•toh

For Numbers, see page 167.

Telephone Etiquette

Hello. This is…	**Hola. Soy…** *oh•lah soy…*
Can I speak to…?	**¿Puedo hablar con…?** *pweh•doh ah•blahr kohn…*
Extension…	**Extensión…** *ehx•tehn•seeyohn…*
Speak louder/more slowly, please.	**Hable más alto/despacio, por favor.** *ah•bleh mahs*
	ahl•toh/dehs•pah•seeyoh pohr fah•bohr
Can you repeat that?	**¿Puede repetir eso?** *pweh•deh rreh•peh•teer eh•soh*
I'll call back later.	**Llamaré más tarde.** *yah•mah•reh mahs tahr•deh*
Bye.	**Adiós.** *ah•deeyohs*

YOU MAY HEAR...

¿Quién habla? *keeyehn ah•blah*	Who's calling?
Espere. *ehs•peh•reh*	Hold on.
Le comunico. *leh coh•muh•nee•coh*	I'll put you through.
El/Ella no está aquí/está en otra línea *ehl/e•jah no eh•stah a•kee/eh•stah ehn oh•trah leen•yah*	He/She is not here/on another line.
¿Quiere dejarle un mensaje? *keeyeh•reh deh•khahr•leh oon mehn•sah•kheh*	Would you like to leave a message?
Vuelva a llamar más tarde/en diez minutos. *bwehl•bah ah yah•mahr mahs tahr•deh/ehn deeyehs mee•noo•tohs*	Call back later/in ten minutes.
¿Quiere que le devuelva la llamada? *keeyeh•reh keh leh deh•bwehl•bah lah yah•mah•dah*	Can he/she call you back?
¿Me da su número? *meh dah soo noo•meh•roh*	What's your number?

Public phones in Mexico are coin or card operated, but they are a rare sight these days. Phone cards can be purchased at newsstands and supermarkets. There is good cell phone coverage in most of the country; **GSM** is the most widely used system. For international calls, prepaid calling cards are the most economical option and are available at most newsstands. You can also make long-distance calls at **centros de negocios** (business centers). The latter also offer internet, fax and wireless phone-charging services at reasonable prices. Calling internationally from your hotel may be convenient, but the rates can be very expensive. To call the U.S. or Canada from Mexico, dial 00 + 1 + area code + phone number. To call the U.K. from Mexico, dial 00 + 44 + area code (minus the first 0) + phone number.

Fax

Can I send/receive a fax here?	**¿Puedo enviar/recibir un fax aquí?**
	pweh·doh ehn·bee·ahr/reh·see·beer oon fahx ah·kee
What's the fax number?	**¿Cuál es el número de fax?**
	kwahl ehs ehl noo·meh·roh deh fahx
Please fax this to...	**Por favor envíe este fax a...**
	pohr fah·bohr ehn·bee·eh ehs·teh fahx ah...

Post

Where's the post office/mailbox?	**¿Dónde está la oficina/el buzón de correos?**
	dohn·deh ehs·tah lah oh·fee·see·nah/ehl boo·sohn deh koh·rreh·ohs
A stamp for this postcard/letter to...	**Una estampilla para esta postal/carta a...**
	oo·nah ehs·tahm·pee·yah pah·rah ehs·tah pohs·tahl/kahr·tah ah...

How much?	**¿Cuánto es?** kwahn•toh ehs
Send this package by airmail/express.	**Quiero mandar este paquete por correo aéreo/ urgente.** keeyeh•roh mahn•dahr ehs•teh pah•keh•teh pohr koh•rreh•oh ah•eh•reh•oh/oor•khen•teh
A receipt, please.	**Un comprobante, por favor.** oon kohn•proh•bahn•teh pohr fah•bohr

YOU MAY HEAR...

Llene la declaración aduanal. yeh•neh lah deh•klah•rah•seeyohn ah•dwah•nahl	Fill out the customs declaration form.
¿Qué valor tiene? keh bah•lohr teeyeh•neh	What's the value?
¿Qué hay dentro? keh aye dehn•troh	What's inside?

Las Oficinas de Correos (post offices) offer standard postal services. The Mexican Post Office offers a service called **MEXPOST** for national and international deliveries.

Food & Drink

Eating Out 57

Meals & Cooking 66

Drinks 81

On the Menu 85

Eating Out

ESSENTIAL

Can you recommend a good restaurant/bar?	**¿Puede recomendarme un buen restaurante/ bar?** *pweh·deh rreh·koh·mehn·dahr·meh oon bwehn rrehs·taw·rahn·teh/bahr*
Is there a traditional /an inexpensive restaurant nearby?	**¿Hay un restaurante típico/barato cerca de aquí?** *aye oon rrehs·taw·rahn·teh tee·pee·koh/ bah·rah·toh sehr·kah deh ah·kee*
A table for..., please.	**Una mesa para..., por favor.** *oo·nah meh·sah pah·rah...pohr fah·bohr*
Can we sit...?	**¿Podemos sentarnos...?** *poh·deh·mohs sehn·tahr·nohs...*
here/there	**aquí/allá** *ah·kee/ah·yah*
outside	**afuera** *ah·fweh·rah*
in a non-smoking area	**en el área de no fumar** *ehn ehl ah·reh·ah deh noh foo·mahr*
I'm waiting for someone.	**Estoy esperando a alguien.** *ehs·toy ehs·peh·rahn·doh ah ahl·geeyehn*
Where are the toilets?	**¿Dónde está el baño?** *dohn·deh ehs·tah ehl bah·nyo*
The menu, please.	**Un menú, por favor.** *oon meh·noo pohr fah·bohr*
What do you recommend?	**¿Qué me recomienda?** *keh meh rreh·koh·meeyehn·dah*
I'd like...	**Quiero...** *keeyeh·roh...*
Some more..., please.	**Quiero más..., por favor.** *keeyeh·roh mahs...pohr fah·bohr*
Enjoy your meal!	**¡Buen provecho!** *bwen proh·beh·choh*
The check [bill], please.	**La cuenta, por favor.** *lah kwen·tah pohr fah·bohr*

Is service included?	**¿Está incluido el cubierto?**
	ehs·tah een·kloo·ee·doh ehl koo·beeyehr·toh
Can I pay by credit card/have a receipt?	**¿Puedo pagar con tarjeta de crédito?/**
	¿Podría darme un comprobante? *pweh·doh*
	pah·gahr kohn tahr·kheh·tah deh kreh·dee·toh/
	poh·dree·ah dahr·meh oon kohm·proh·bahn·teh

Where to Eat

Can you recommend…?	**¿Puede recomendarme…?**
	pweh·deh rreh·koh·mehn·dahr·meh…
a restaurant	**un restaurante** *oon rrehs·taw·rahn·teh*
a bar	**un bar** *oon bahr*
a café	**una cafetería** *oonah kah·feh·teh·reeah*
a fast food place	**un restaurante de comida rápida**
	oon rrehs·taw·rahn·teh deh koh·mee·dah
	rrah·pee·dah
a cheap restaurant	**un restaurante barato**
	oon rrehs·taw·rahn·teh bahrahto
an expensive restaurant	**un restaurante caro**
	oon rrehs·taw·rahn·teh kahroh
a restaurant with a good view	**un restaurante con buena vista**
	oon rrehs·taw·rahn·teh kohn buenah vistah
an authentic/a non touristy restaurant	**un restaurante típico no turístico**
	oon rrehs·taw·rahn·teh teepeekoh noh tooreesteekoh

Reservations & Preferences

I'd like to reserve a table…	**Quiero reservar una mesa…**
	keeyeh·roh rreh·sehr·bahr oo·nah meh·sah…
for two	**para dos** *pah·rah dohs*
for this evening	**para esta noche** *pah·rah ehs·tah noh·cheh*

for tomorrow at…	**para mañana a la/las…**
	pah•rah mah•nyah•nah ah lah/lahs…
A table for two, please.	**Una mesa para dos, por favor.**
	oo•nah meh•sah pah•rah dohs pohr fah•bohr
We have a reservation.	**Tenemos una reservación.**
	teh•neh•mohs oo•nah rreh•sehr•bah•seeohn
My name is…	**Me llamo…**
	meh yah•moh…
Can we sit…?	**¿Podríamos sentarnos…?**
	poh•dree•ah•mohs sehn•tahr•nohs…
here/there	**aquí/allá**
	ah•kee/ah•ya
outside	**afuera** *ah•fweh•rah*
in a non smoking area	**en el área de no fumar ehn**
	ehl ah•reh•ah deh noh foo•mahr
by the window	**junto a la ventana**
	khoon•toh ah lah behn•tah•nah
in the shade	**en la sombra** *ehn lah sohmbrah*
in the sun	**en el sol** *ehn ehl sohl*
Where are the toilets?	**¿Dónde está el baño?**
	dohn•deh ehs•tah ehl bah•nyoh

YOU MAY HEAR...

¿Tiene reservación?
teeyeh·neh rreh·sehr·bah·see·ohn

Do you have a reservation?

¿Cuántos son?
kwahn·tohs sohn

How many?

¿En el área de fumar o no fumar?
ehn ehl ah·reh·ah deh foo·mahr oh noh foo·mahr

Smoking or non-smoking?

¿Está listo *m* /lista *f* para ordenar?
ehs·tah lees·toh /lees·tah pah·rah ohr·deh·nahr

Are you ready (to order)?

¿Qué va a ordenar?
keh bah ah orh·deh·nahr

What would you like?

Le recomiendo...
leh reh·koh·meeyehn·doh...

I recommend...

Buen provecho. *bwen proh·beh·choh*

Enjoy your meal.

How to Order

Excuse me, sir/ma'am?	**¿Disculpe, señor/señorita/señora?**	
	Dis·kool·peh, sehn·hior/sehn·hior·i·tah/sehn·hio·ra?	
We're ready (to order).	**Estamos listos para ordenar.**	
	ehs·tah·mohs lees·tohs pah·rah ohr·deh·nahr	
The wine list, please.	**La carta de vinos, por favor.**	
	lah kahr·tah deh bee·nohs pohr fah·bohr	
I'd like...	**Quiero...** *keeyeh·roh...*	
a bottle of...	**una botella de...** *oo·nah boh·teh·yah deh...*	
a carafe of...	**una jarra de...** *oo·nah khah·rrah deh...*	
a glass of...	**una copa de...** *oonah koh·pah deh...*	
The menu, please.	**La carta, por favor.** *lah kahr·tah pohr fah·bohr*	
Do you have...?	**¿Tiene...?** *teeyeh·neh...*	

a menu in English	**un menú en inglés**	*oon meh•noo ehn een•glehs*
a fixed price menu	**el menú del día**	*ehl meh•noo dehl dee•ah*
a children's menu	**un menú para niños**	*oon meh•noo pah•rah nee•nyohs*
What do you recommend?	**¿Qué me recomienda?** *keh meh rreh•koh•meeyehn•dah*	
What's this?	**¿Qué es esto?** *keh ehs ehs•toh*	
What's in it?	**¿Qué lleva?** *keh yeh•bah*	
Is it spicy?	**¿Es picante?** *ehs pee•kahn•teh*	
Without…, please.	**Sin…, por favor.** *seen… pohr fah•bohr*	
It's to go [take away].	**Es para llevar.** *ehs pah•rah yeh•bahr*	

For Drinks, see page 81.

61

YOU MAY SEE…

SE COBRA COVER	cover charge
PRECIO FIJO	fixed price
MENÚ DEL DÍA	menu (of the day)
CUBIERTO (NO) INCLUIDO	service (not) included
ESPECIALIDADES DE LA CASA	specials

Cooking Methods

baked	**al horno**	*ahl ohr•noh*
barbecued	**a la parrilla**	*ah lah parrihjah*
boiled	**hervido** *m* /**hervida** *f* *ehr•bee•doh/ehr•bee•dah*	
braised	**a fuego lento**	*ah fweh•goh lehn•toh*
breaded	**empanizado** *m* /**empanizada** *f*	
	ehm•pah•nee•sah•doh/ehm•pah•nee•sah•dah	
creamed	**con crema**	*kohn kreh•mah*
diced	**cortado en cuadritos**	
	kohr•tah•doh ehn kwah•dree•tohs	

filleted	**fileteado** *fee·leh·teh·ah·doh*
fried/ deep-fried	**frito** m **/frita** f *free·toh/free·tah*
grilled	**a la plancha** *ah lah plahn·chah*
poached	**escalfado** m **/escalfada** f *ehs·kahl·fah·doh /ehs·kahl·fah·dah*
roasted	**asado** m **/asada** f *ah·sah·doh/ah·sah·dah*
sautéed	**salteado** m **/salteada** f *sahl·teh·ah·doh/sahl·teh·ah·dah*
smoked	**ahumado** m**/ahumada** f *ah·oo·mah·doh/ah·oo·mah·dah*
steamed	**al vapor** *ahl bah·pohr*
stewed	**guisado** m **/guisada** f *gee·sah·doh/gee·sah·dah*
stir-fried	**salteado** *sahltehahdoh*
stuffed	**relleno** m **/rellena** f *rreh·yeh·noh /rreh·yeh·nah*

Dietary Requirements

I'm...	**Soy...** *soy...*
diabetic	**diabético** m **/diabética** f *deeyah·beh·tee·koh / deeyah·beh·tee·kah*
lactose intolerant	**intolerante a la lactosa** *een·toh·leh·rahn·teh ah lah lahk·toh·sah*
vegetarian	**vegetariano** m **/vegetariana** f *beh·kheh·tah·reeyah·noh/beh·kheh·tah·reeyah·nah*
vegan	**vegano/vegana** *beh·gah·noh/ beh·gah·nah*
I'm allergic to...	**Soy alérgico** m **/alérgica** f **a...** *soy ah·lehr·khee·koh/ah·lehr·khee·kah ah...*
I can't eat...	**No puedo comer...** *noh pweh·doh koh·mehr...*
dairy products	**productos lácteos** *proh·dook·tohs lahk·teh·ohs*
gluten	**gluten** *gloo·tehn*
nuts	**nueces** *noo·eh·sehs*
pork	**carne de puerco** *kahr·neh deh pwehr·koh*

shellfish	**mariscos** *mah·rees·kohs*
spicy foods	**comidas picantes** *koh·mee·dahs pee·kahn·tehs*
wheat	**trigo** *tree·goh*
Is it halal/kosher?	**¿Es halal/kosher?** *ehs ah·lahl/koh·shehr*
Do you have…?	**¿Tiene…?** *Tee·ehneh*
skimmed milk	**leche descremada** *leh·cheh dehs·kreh·mah·dah*
whole milk	**leche entera** *leh·cheh ehn·teh·rah*
soya milk	**leche de soya** *leh·cheh deh soh·yah*

Dining with Children

Do you have children's portions?	**¿Sirven raciones para niños?** *seer·behn rrah·seeyoh·nehs pah·rah nee·nyohs*
A highchair/child's seat, please.	**Una periquera/silla para niños, por favor.** *oo·nah peh·ree·keh·rah/see·yah pah·rah nee·nyohs pohr fah·bohr*
Where can I feed/ change the baby?	**¿Dónde puedo darle de comer/cambiar al niño?** *dohn·deh pweh·doh dahr·leh deh koh·mehr/ kahm·beeyahr ahl nee·nyoh*
Can you warm this?	**¿Puede calentar esto?** *pweh·deh kah·lehn·tahr ehs·toh*

For Traveling with Children, see page 143.

How to Complain

When will our food be ready?	**¿Cuándo estará lista nuestra comida?**
	Cuahn·doh esta·hrah lees·tah nuehs·trah koh·midah?
We can't wait any longer.	**No podemos esperar más.**
	noh poh·deh·mohs ehs·peh·rahr mahs
We're leaving.	**Nos vamos.**
	nohs bah·mohs
I didn't order this.	**Esto no es lo que ordené.**
	ehs·toh noh ehs loh keh ohr·deh·neh
I ordered…	**Pedí…** *peh·dee…*
I can't eat this.	**No puedo comerme esto.**
	noh pweh·doh koh·mehr·meh ehs·toh
This is too…	**Esto está demasiado…**
	ehs·toh ehs·tah deh·mah·seeyah·doh…
cold/hot	**frío/caliente**
	free·oh/kah·leeyehn·teh
salty/spicy	**salado/picante**
	sah·lah·doh/pee·kahn·teh
tough/bland	**duro/insípido** *doo·roh/een·see·pee·doh*
This isn't clean/fresh.	**Esto no está limpio/fresco.**
	ehs·toh noh ehs·tah leem·peeyoh/frehs·koh

Paying

The check [bill], please.	**La cuenta, por favor.**
	lah kwehn·tah pohr fah·bohr
Separate checks [bills], please.	**Cuentas separadas, por favor.**
	kwehn·tahs seh·pah·rah·dahs pohr fah·bohr
It's all together.	**Póngalo todo junto.**
	pohn·gah·loh toh·doh khoon·toh
Is service included?	**¿Está incluido el cubierto?**
	ehs·tah een·kloo·ee·doh ehl koo·beeyehr·toh

What's this amount for?	**¿De qué es esta cantidad?** *deh keh ehs ehs•tah kahn•tee•dahd*
I didn't have that. I had…	**Yo no ordené eso. Tomé…** *yoh noh ohr•deh•neh eh•soh toh•meh…*
Can I have a receipt/ an itemized bill?	**¿Podría darme un comprobante/una cuenta detallada?** *poh•dree•ah dahr•meh oon kohm•proh•bahn•teh/oo•nah kwehn•tah deh•tah•yah•dah*
That was delicious!	**¡Estuvo delicioso!** *ehs•too•boh deh•lee•seeyoh•soh*
I've already paid.	**Ya pagué.** *Jah pah•geh*

Meals & Cooking

El desayuno (breakfast) is usually served from 7:00 a.m. to 10:00 a.m. **La comida** (lunch), generally the largest meal of the day, is served from 1:00 p.m. to 4:00 p.m. **La cena** (dinner) is typically smaller and lighter than in the U.S. or U.K., and is usually served after 8:00 p.m.

Breakfast

Tocino *toh•cee•noh*	bacon
la mantequilla *lah mahn•teh•kee•yah*	butter
el café/el té... *ehl kah•feh/ehl teh...*	coffee/tea...
solo *soh•loh*	black
descafeinado *dehs•kah•feh•ee•nah•doh*	decaf
con leche *kohn leh•cheh*	with milk
con azúcar *kohn ah•soo•kahr*	with sugar
con endulzante artificial *kohn ehn•dool•sahn•teh ahr•tee•fee•seeyahl*	with artificial sweetener
los cereales (calientes/fríos) *lohs seh•reh•ah•lehs (kah•leeyehn•tehs/free•ohs)*	cold/hot cereal
las carnes frías *lahs kahr•nehs free•ahs*	cold cuts
el cruasán *ehl crooah•sahn*	le croissant
la mermelada/la jalea *lah mehr•meh•lah•dah/khah•leh•ah*	jam/jelly
el queso *ehl keh•soh*	cheese
el jugo *ehl khoo•goh*	...juice
naranja *nah•rahn•ha*	orange

manzana *mahn·sah·nah*	apple
toronja *toh·rohn·hah*	grapefriut
la leche *lah leh·cheh*	milk
la avena *lah ah·beh·nah*	oatmeal
el agua *ehl ah·gwah*	water
granola *grah·noh·lah*	granola [muesli]
panqué *pahn·keh*	muffin
el huevo... *ehl weh·boh...*	...egg
duro/tibio *doo·roh/tee·beeyoh*	hard /soft boiled
frito *free·toh*	fried
revuelto *rreh·bwehl·toh*	scrambled
el omelet... *ehl oh·meh·leht...*	omelet
el pan *ehl pahn*	bread
el pan tostado *ehl pahn tohs·tah·doh*	toast
bollo *boh·joh*	roll
la salchicha *lah sahl·chee·chah*	sausage
el yogur *ehl yoh·goor*	yogurt

Appetizers

las chalupas *lahs chah·loo·pahs*	tortillas with potato, chicken, onion and salsa topping
el chicharrón *ehl chee·chah·rrohn*	deep fried pork skin

los frijoles refritos
lohs free·khoh·lehs rreh·free·tohs
mashed and fried black beans

las gorditas *lahs gohr·dee·tahs*
little corn cakes baked or fried

el guacamole *ehl gwa·hkah·moh·leh*
mashed avocado, onions, tomatoes and lime juice

las quesadillas *lahs keh·sah·dee·yahs*
corn tortillas stuffed with cheese, beef, chicken, etc.

el queso fundido *ehl keh·soh foon·dee·doh*
Mexican fondue

la salsa *lah sahl·sah*
chopped or pureed tomatoes, chiles, onions and cilantro

los tacos *lohs tah·kohs*
soft tortillas filled with a variety of meat and vegetables

la tortilla *lah tohr·tee·yah*
thin, flat bread made of corn

Soup

caldo tlalpeño *kahl·doh tlahl·peh·nyo*
soup made with vegetables, chicken and sometimes rice

crema *creh·mah*
soup made with cream and assorted ingredients

pozole *poh·soh·leh*
soup of stewed pork and corn kernels, garnished with lettuce, horseradish and oregano

sopa de lima *soh·pah deh lee·mah lima*
(citrus fruit) soup with seasoned chicken broth

sopa de tortilla *soh·pah deh tohr·tee·yah*
tomato broth garnished with fried tortilla strips, cream, avocado, cheese, chili and pork skin

Fish & Seafood

las almejas *lahs ahl·meh·khahs*	clam
las anchoas *lahs ahn·choh·ahs*	fresh baby anchovy
los calamares fritos *lohs kah·lah·mah·rehs free·tohs*	deep-fried squid
el arenque *ehl ah·rehn·keh*	herring
el atún *ehl ah·toon*	tuna
el bacalao *ehl bah·kah·la·oh*	cod
el besugo *ehl beh·soo·goh*	sea bream
los callos de hacha *lohs kah·yohs deh ah·chah*	scallops
el cangrejo *ehl kahn·greh·khoh*	crab
el cazón *ehl kah·sohn*	baby shark
el acocil *ehl ah·koh·seel*	crayfish
los langostinos *lohs lahn·gohs·tee·nohs*	prawn
la langosta *lah lahn·gohs·tah*	lobster
el lenguado *ehl lehn·gwah·doh*	sole
el robalo *ehl roh·bah·loh*	sea bass
los mejillones *lohs meh·khee·yoh·nehs*	mussels
los mejillones en escabeche *lohs meh·khee·yohn·ehs ehn ehs·kah·beh·cheh*	mussels in a marinade
la merluza *lah mehr·loo·sah*	hake

el mero *ehl meh·roh*	grouper
la sierra *lah see·eh·rrah*	mackerel
el ostión *lah ohs·tee·ohn*	oyster
el pámpano *ehl pahm·pah·noh*	yellowtail
el pez espada *ehl pehs ehs·pah·dah*	swordfish
el pulpo *ehl pool·poh*	octopus
el pulpo al olivo	octopus with olive
ehl pool·poh ahl oh·lee·boh	
el salmón *ehl sahl·mohn*	salmon
el tiburón *ehl tee·boo·rohn*	shark
la mojarra *lah moh·khah·rrah*	tilapia
la trucha *lah troo·chah*	trout
la trucha ahumada	smoked trout
lah troo·chah aw·mah·dah	

Ceviche is made by marinating raw fish with lime. The citrus adds flavor and cooks the fish without heat. The preparation includes chopped onions, tomato and olives, with a dash of hot salsa. **Ceviche** is served cold, accompanied by crackers.

ceviche... *seh·bee·cheh...*	marinated, raw...
de callos de hacha	scallops
deh kah·yohs deh ah·chah	
de camarones *deh kah·mah·roh·nehs*	shrimp
de langostinos *deh lahn·gohs·tee·nohs*	prawn
de mariscos *deh mah·rees·kohs*	mixed seafood
de pescado *deh pehs·kah·do*	fish
de pulpo *deh pool·poh*	octopus

Meat & Poultry

La tira de carne *lah tee·rah deh cahr·neh* — strip steak

el bistec *ehl bees·tehk* — beefsteak

el cabrito *ehl kah·bree·toh* — kid (young goat)

la carne *lah kahr·neh* — meat

la carne de puerco
lah kahr·neh deh pwehr·koh — pork

la carne de res *lah kahr·neh deh rehs* — beef

la carne molida *lah kahr·neh moh·lee·dah* — ground beef

el chorizo *ehl choh·ree·soh* — chorizo pork sausage

la chuleta *lah choo·leh·tah* — chop

la codorniz *lah koh·dohr·nees* — quail

el conejo *ehl koh·neh·khoh* — rabbit

el cordero *ehl kohr·deh·roh* — lamb

las costillas de puerco
lahs kohs·tee·yahs deh pwehr·koh — pork ribs

la falda *lah fahl·dah* — beef flank steak

el filete *ehl fee·leh·teh* — steak

el hígado... *ehl ee·gah·doh...* — ...liver

   de cordero *deh kohr·deh·roh* — lamb

   de pollo *deh poh·yoh* — chicken

   de res *deh rrehs* — beef

el jamón *ehl khah·mohn* — ham

el jamón serrano
ehl khah·mohn seh·rrah·noh — dry-cured serrano ham

el lomo *ehl loh·moh* — loin

las mollejas de ternera *lahs moh·yeh·khahs deh tehr·neh·rah* — veal sweetbread

la moronga *lah moh·rohn·gah* — blood sausage

las patas de puerco
lahs pah·tahs deh pwehr·koh — pig's feet [trotters]

el pato *ehl pah·toh*	duck
el pavo *ehl pah·boh*	turkey
el pollo *ehl poh·yoh*	chicken
el pollo frito *ehl poh·yoh free·toh*	fried chicken
el riñón *ehl rree·nyohn*	kidney
la riñonada *lah rree·nyo·nah·dah*	kidney stew
la salchicha *lah sahl·chee·chah*	sausage
el salchichón *ehl sahl·chee·chohn*	salami-type sausage
el sirloin *ehl seer·loh·een*	sirloin
la ternera *lah tehr·neh·rah*	veal
el tocino *ehl toh·see·noh*	bacon
el venado *ehl beh·nah·doh*	venison

Meat dishes are popular in Mexico, and the northern states of **Sonora** and **Chihuahua** are famous for their cuts of beef. Traditional dishes include **carne asada** (grilled meat), which is usually served with a side of tortillas, beans, grilled onions and salsa. Another Mexican specialty is the **barbacoa:** mutton cooked in the ground with spices and wrapped in maguey leaves. The resulting broth is seasoned and served as a soup.

The **torta**, which is basically a sandwich made with a kind of white bread, is also a specialty. These are filled with **frijoles refritos** (mashed and fried black beans), meat, lettuce, tomato, onion and chili, among other things. They can have many ingredients or just a few, depending on each person's taste.

Vegetables & Staples

la aceituna *lah ah·seyee·too·nah*	olive
la acelga *lah ah·sehl·gah*	chard
el aguacate *ehl ah·gwah·khah·teh*	avocado
el ajo *ehl ah·khoh*	garlic
la alcachofa *lah ahl·kah·choh·fah*	artichoke
el apio *ehl ah·peeyoh*	celery
la berenjena *lah beh·rehn·kheh·nah*	eggplant [aubergine]
el brócoli *ehl broh·koh·lee*	broccoli
el calabacita *lah kah·lah·bah·see·tah*	zucchini [courgette]
el camote *ehl kah·moh·teh*	yam
la cebolla *lah seh·boh·yah*	onion
el champiñón *ehl chahm·pee·nyohn*	mushroom
el chícharo *ehl chee·chah·roh*	green pea
el chile *ehl chee·leh*	hot pepper
el chile chipotle *ehl chee·leh chee·poh·tleh*	chipotle pepper
el chile jalapeño *ehl chee·leh khah·lah·peh·nyo*	jalapeño pepper
el chile verde *ehl chee·leh behr·deh*	hot green pepper
la col *lah kohl*	cabbage
la coliflor *lah koh·lee·flohr*	cauliflower

el ejote *ehl eh•khoh•teh*	green bean
el espárrago *ehl ehs•pah•rrah•goh*	asparagus
la espinaca *lah ehs•pee•nah•kah*	spinach
los frijoles *lah free•kho•lehs*	beans
el germen de soya *ehl gehr•mehn deh soh•yah*	bean sprouts
las habas *lahs ah•bahs*	broad beans
la harina *lah ah•ree•nah*	flour
el jitomate *ehl khee•toh•mah•teh*	tomato
la lechuga *lah leh•choo•gah*	lettuce
la lenteja *lah lehn•teh•khah*	lentil
el maíz *ehl mah•ees*	corn
la papa *lah pah•pah*	potato
el pepino *ehl peh•pee•noh*	cucumber

Fruit

el arándano azul ehl *ah•rahn•dah•noh ah•sool*	blueberry
el arándano rojo *ehl ah•rahn•dah•noh roh•khoh*	cranberry
la cereza *lah seh•reh•sah*	cherry
el chabacano *ehl chah•bah•kah•noh*	apricot
la chirimoya *lah chee•ree•moh•yah*	custard apple
la ciruela *lah see•rweh•lah*	plum
el coco *ehl koh•koh*	coconut
el durazno *ehl duh•rahs•noh*	peach
la frambuesa *lah frahm•bweh•sah*	raspberry
la fresa *lah freh•sah*	strawberry
la fruta *lah froo•tah*	fruit
la granada roja *lah grah•nah•dah roh•khah*	pomegranate
la guayaba *lah gwah•yah•bah*	guava

el kiwi *ehl kee•wee*	kiwi
el limón *ehl lee•mohn*	lime
el limón amarillo *ehl lee•mohn ah•mah•ree•yoh*	lemon
el mamey *ehl mah•mehy*	mamey (type of tropical fruit)
el mango *ehl mahn•goh*	mango
la mandarina *lah mahn•dah•ree•nah*	tangerine
la manzana *lah mahn•sah•nah*	apple
el maracuyá *ehl mah•rah•coo•yah*	passion fruit
el melón *ehl meh•lohn*	melon
la naranja *lah nah•rahn•khah*	orange
la nectarina *lah nehk•tah•ree•nah*	nectarine
la papaya *lah pah•pah•yah*	papaya
la pera *lah peh•rah*	pear
la piña *lah pee•nyah*	pineapple
el plátano *ehl plah•tah•noh*	banana
la sandía *lah sahn•dee•ah*	watermelon
el tamarindo *ehl tah•mah•reen•doh*	tamarind
la toronja *lah toh•rohn•khah*	grapefruit
la uva *lah oo•bah*	grape

One of Mexico's most widely enjoyed culinary exports is **chocolate**. **Chocolate** is made from **cacao**, and has been enjoyed in various forms for the last three thousand years. You'll find that Mexican chocolate is usually dark and is combined with sugar, cinnamon and often nuts. Another specialty is **cajeta**, caramelized cow's or goat's milk. It is a traditional Mexican sweet that may be enjoyed on its own or as a topping for pastries, bread and even ice cream.

Dessert

el arroz con leche
ehl ah·rrohs kohn leh·cheh

rice pudding

el ate *ehl ah·teh*

fruit and sugar dessert

el rollo de pastel
roh·yoh deh pahs·tehl khee· tah·noh

sponge cake roll
with cream filling

el buñuelo *ehl boo·nyweh·loh*

thin, deep-fried fritter,
covered in sugar

la cajeta *lah kah·kheh·tah*

cooked goat's milk with sugar

el churro *ehl choo·rroh*

deep-fried fritter
sprinkled with sugar

la crepa *lah kreh·pah*

crepe (used in sweet
or savory dishes)

el flan *ehl flahn*

caramel custard

la galleta *lah gah·yeh·tah*

cookie [biscuit]

la gelatina *lah kheh·lah·tee·nah*

gelatin dessert

el helado *ehl eh·lah·doh*

ice cream

la natilla *lah nah·tee·yah*

fried milk custard

la mantecada *lah mahn·teh·kah·dah*

small sponge cake

la manzana horneada   baked apple
lah mahn·sah·nah ohr·neh·ah·dah

la nieve *lah nyeh·beh*   sorbet

la palanqueta *lah pah·lahn·keh·tah*   kind of peanut butter

el pay de manzana   apple pie
ehl pahee deh mahn·sah·nah

el pay de limón *ehl pahee deh lee·mohn*   key lime pie

el pay de queso *ehl pahee deh keh·soh*   cheesecake

Cheese

el queso... *ehl keh·soh...*   ...cheese

    añejo *ah·nyeh·khoh*   ripe

    manchego *mahn·cheh·goh*   mild-flavored, essential for making quesadillas

    chihuahua *chee·wah·wah*   yellow

    crema *kreh·mah*   cream

    de leche de cabra   goat's milk
    deh leh·cheh deh kah·brah

    duro *doo·roh*   hard

    fuerte *fwehr·teh*   strong

    jalapeño *khah·lah·peh·nyo*   jalapeño pepper

    oaxaca *oh·ah·khah·kah*   similar to mozzarella

    panela *pah·neh·lah*   white

    parmesano *pahr·meh·sah·noh*   parmesan

    rallado *rrah·yah·doh*   grated

    requesón *rreh·keh·sohn*   similar to ricotta

Sauces & Condiments

ketchup	**catsup** *kaht·soop*	
mustard	**mostaza** *mohs·tah·sah*	
black pepper	**la pimienta negra** *lah pee·meeyehn·tah neh·grah*	
salt	**sal** *sahl*	

At the Market

Where are the trolleys/ baskets?	**¿Dónde están los carritos/las canastas?**	*dohn·deh ehs·tahn lohs kah·rree·tohs/lahs kah·nahs·tahs*
Where is…?	**¿Donde está…?**	*dohn·deh ehs·tah…*
I'd like some of that/this.	**Quiero un poco de eso/esto.**	*keeyeh·roh oon poh·koh deh eh·soh/ehs·toh*
Can I taste it?	**¿Puedo probarlo?**	*pweh·doh proh·bahr·loh*
I'd like…	**Quiero…**	*keeyeh·roh…*
a kilo/half kilo of…	**un kilo/medio kilo de…**	*oon kee·loh/ meh·deeyoh kee·loh deh…*
a liter of…	**un litro de…**	*oon lee·troh deh…*
a piece of…	**un trozo de…**	*oon troh·soh deh…*
a slice of…	**una rebanada de…**	*oo·nah reh·bah·nah·dah deh…*
More./Less.	**Más./Menos.**	*mahs/meh·nohs*
How much?	**¿Cuánto es?**	*kwahn·toh ehs*
Where do I pay?	**¿Dónde pago?**	*dohn·deh pah·goh*
A bag, please.	**Una bolsa, por favor.**	*oo·nah bohl·sah pohr fah·bohr*
I'm being helped.	**Ya me están atendiendo.**	*yah meh ehs·tahn ah·tehn·deeyehn·doh*

For Conversion Tables, see page 171.

In Mexico, food is often purchased at local family-run markets or farmer's markets. These are excellent places for regional and specialty food such as fresh fruit and vegetables, meat and baked goods. **Supermercados** (supermarkets) are also common, but these are usually found only in big cities. These stores have a larger selection than regular markets, and can be less expensive.

YOU MAY HEAR...

¿Necesita ayuda? *neh·seh·see·tah ah·yoo·dah*   Can I help you?

¿Qué desea? *keh deh·seh·ah?*   What would you like?

¿Algo más? *ahl·goh mahs*   Anything else?

Son…pesos. *sohn…peh·sohs*   That's…pesos.

Measurements in Mexico are **metric** and that applies to the weight of food too. If you tend to think in pounds and ounces, it's worth brushing up on what the metric equivalent is before you go shopping for fruit and veg in markets and supermarkets. Five hundred grams, or half a kilo, is a common quantity to order, and that converts to just over a pound (17.65 ounces, to be precise).

YOU MAY SEE...

CONSUMIR PREFERENTEMENTE ANTES DE...	best if used by...
CALORÍAS	calories
SIN GRASA	fat free
MANTENER REFRIGERADO	keep refrigerated
PUEDE CONTENER RASTROS DE...	may contain traces of...
APTO PARA MICROONDAS	microwaveable
VENDER HASTA...	sell by...
APTO PARA VEGETARIANOS	suitable for vegetarians

In the Kitchen

bottle opener	**el destapador** *ehl dehs·tah·pah·dohr*
bowl	**el tazón** *ehl tah·sohn*
can opener	**el abrelatas** *ehl ah·breh·lah·tahs*
corkscrew	**el sacacorchos** *ehl sah·kah·kohr·chohs*
cup	**la taza** *lah tah·sah*
fork	**el tenedor** *ehl teh·neh·dohr*
frying pan	**el sartén** *ehl sahr·tehn*
glass	**el vaso** *ehl bah·soh*
(steak) knife	**el cuchillo** *ehl koo·chee·yoh (deh kahr·neh)*
measuring cup/spoon	**taza/cuchara para medir** *tah·sah/cu·chah·rah pah·rah meh·deer*
napkin	**la servilleta** *lah sehr·bee·yeh·tah*
plate	**el plato** *ehl plah·toh*
pot	**la olla** *lah oh·yah*
spatula	**la espátula** *lah ehs·pah·too·lah*
spoon	**la cuchara** *lah koo·chah·rah*

Drinks

ESSENTIAL

The wine list/drink menu, please.	**La carta de vinos/bebidas, por favor.** *lah kahr·tah deh bee·nohs/beh·bee·dahs pohr fah·bohr*
What do you recommend?	**¿Qué me recomienda?** *keh meh rreh·koh·meeyehn·dah*
I'd like a bottle/glass of red/white wine.	**Quiero una botella/una copa de vino tinto/blanco.** *keeyeh·roh oo·nah boh·teh·yah/oo·nah koh·pah deh bee·noh teen·toh/blahn·koh*
The house wine, please.	**El vino de la casa, por favor.** *ehl bee·noh deh lah kah·sah pohr fah·bohr*
Another bottle/glass, please.	**Otra botella/copa, por favor.** *oh·trah boh·teh·yah/koh·pah pohr fah·bohr*
I'd like a local beer.	**Quiero una cerveza nacional.** *keeyeh·roh oo·nah sehr·beh·sah nah·seeoh·nhal*
Can I buy you a drink?	**¿Puedo invitarle una copa?** *pweh·doh een·bee·tahr·leh oo·nah koh·pah*
Cheers!	**¡Salud!** *sah·lood*
A coffee/tea, please.	**Un café/té, por favor.** *oon kah·feh/teh pohr fah·bohr*
Black.	**Solo.** *soh·loh*
With...	**Con...** *kohn...*
milk	**leche** *leh·cheh*
sugar	**azúcar** *ah·soo·kahr*
artificial sweetener	**endulzante artificial** *ehn·dool·sahn·teh ahr·tee·fee·seeyahl*
A..., please.	**..., por favor.** *...pohr fah·bohr*
juice	**Un jugo** *khoo·goh*
soda	**Un refresco** *rreh·frehs·koh*
(sparkling/still) water	**Un agua (con/sin gas)** *ah·gwah (kohn/ seen gahs)*

There are many popular brands of Mexican beer, such as
Corona®, Sol®, Tecate® and **Victoria®**, to name a few. Each
brand usually has several classes and types of beer available, though
most will be a lager-type beer.

Mexican wine is produced in the northern part of the country, with
the **state of Baja California** being the best producer.

Wine routes can be followed in northern Mexico – about 50 wineries,
from small family-owned to mass producers, can be visited. Tours of
the winery and vineyards may be available and some may have on-site
restaurants and shops.

Non-alcoholic Drinks

el agua (con/sin gas)	(sparkling/still) water
ehl ah•gwah (kohn/seen gahs)	
el atole *ehl ah•toh•leh*	a hot drink made from corn
el café *ehl kah•feh*	coffee
el chocolate caliente *ehl*	hot chocolate
choh•koh•lah•teh kah•leeyehn•teh	

el jugo de... *ehl khoo•goh deh. . .*		...juice
manzana *mahn•sah•nah*		apple
naranja *nah•rahn•khah*		orange
toronja *toh•rohn•khah*		grapefruit
la leche *lah leh•cheh*		milk
la limonada *lah lee•moh•nah•dah*		lemonade
la naranjada *lah nah•rahn•khah•dah*		orange soft drink
el sorbete *sohr•beh•teh*		sorbet
el refresco *ehl rreh•frehs•koh*		soda
el té helado *ehl teh eh•lah•doh*		iced tea

Many Mexicans love coffee and drink it throughout the day.
Café de olla is coffee prepared in a clay pot, sweetened with
piloncillo (brown sugar). **Café lechero** is coffee mixed with
steamed milk. Tap water is not always safe to drink. Restaurants often
serve bottled water with meals, unless you specifically request **agua
de la llave** (tap water). Juice is usually served with breakfast, but it's
not common at lunch or dinner.

YOU MAY HEAR...

¿Qué quiere de beber?	Can I get you a drink?
Keh kee•eh•reh deh beh•behr?	
¿Con leche o azúcar?	With milk or sugar?
kohn leh•cheh oh ah•soo•kahr	
¿Agua con gas o sin gas?	Sparkling or still water?
ah•gwah kohn gahs oh seen gahs	

Apéritifs, Cocktails & Liqueurs

el coñac *ehl koh•nyahk* — cognac

la ginebra *lah khee•neh•brah* — gin

el jerez fino *ehl kheh•rehs fee•noh* — pale, dry sherry

el jerez oscuro *ehl kheh•rehs ohs•koo•roh* — dark, heavy sherry

el licor *ehl lee•kohr* — liqueur

el oporto *ehl oh•pohr•toh* — port

el ron *ehl rrohn* — rum

la sangría *lah sahn•gree•ah* — wine punch

el tequila *ehl teh•kee•lah* — tequila

el vodka *ehl bohd•kah* — vodka

el whisky *ehl wees•kee* — whisky

Beer

la cerveza... *lah sehr•beh•sah...* — ...beer

  en botella/de barril — bottled/draft
ehn boh•teh•yah/deh bah•rreel

  nacional/importada — local/imported
nah•seeyoh•nahl/eem•pohr•tah•dah

  oscura/clara *ohs•koo•rah/klah•rah* — dark/light

  rubia *roo•beeyah* — lager

  sin alcohol *seen ahl•koh•ohl* — non-alcoholic

Wine

el vino... *ehl bee•noh...* — ...wine

tinto/blanco *teen•toh/blahn•koh* — red/white

de la casa/de mesa — house/table
deh lah kah•sah/ deh meh•sah

seco/dulce *seh•koh/dool•seh* — dry/sweet

espumoso *ehs•poo•moh•soh* — sparkling

el champán *ehl chahm•pahn* — champagne

On the Menu

la albahaca *lah ahl·bah·kah*	basil
la alcaparra *lah ahl·kah·pah·rrah*	caper
la almendra *lah ahl·mehn·drah*	almond
el anís *ehl ah·nees*	aniseed
el arroz... *ehl ah·rrohs...*	rice...
a la jardinera *ah lah khar·dee·neh·rah*	with corn and peas
a la mexicana *ah lah meh·khee·kah·nah*	with tomatoes and seasoning
blanco *blahn·koh*	white
con frijoles *kohn free·khoh·les*	with beans
con mariscos *kohn mah·rees·kohs*	with seafood
con pollo kohn poh·yoh	with chicken
rojo *rroh·khoh*	red
el azafrán *ehl ah·sah·frahn*	saffron
el azúcar *ehl ah·soo·kahr*	sugar
el aceite *ehl ah·seyee·teh*	oil
el aceite de oliva *ehl ah·seyee·teh deh oh·lee·bah*	olive oil
la acelga *lah ah·sehl·gah*	chard
la achicoria *lah ah·chee·koh·reeyah*	chicory
el agua *ehl ah·gwah*	water
el agua quina *ehl ah·gwa kee·nah*	tonic water
el aguacate *ehl ah·gwah·kah·teh*	avocado
el ajo *ehl ah·khoh*	garlic
el ajonjolí *ehl ah·khphn·kho·lee*	sesame
la albahaca *lah ahl·bah·kah*	basil
la alcachofa *lah ahl·kah·choh·fah*	artichoke
la alcaparra *lah ahl·kah·pah·rrah*	caper
la almeja *lah ahl·meh·khah*	clam
la almendra *lah ahl·mehn·drah*	almond
el jarábe *ehl kha·rha·beh*	syrup

el frijol *ehl free·khohl*	bean
las ancas de rana *lahs ahn·kahs deh rrah·nah*	frog's legs
la anchoa *lah ahn·choh·ah*	anchovy
la angula *lah ahn·goo·lah*	baby eel
el anís *ehl ah·nees*	aniseed
el aperitivo *ehl ah·peh·ree·tee·boh*	appetizer [starter]
el apio *ehl ah·peeyoh*	celery
el arándano azul *ehl ah·rahn·dah·noh ah·sool*	blueberry
el arándano rojo *ehl ah·rahn·dah·noh rroh·khoh*	cranberry
el arenque *ehl ah·rehn·keh*	herring
el arroz *ehl ah·rrohs*	rice
el arroz integral *ehl ah·rrohs een·teh·grahl*	whole grain rice
el arroz salvaje *ehl ah·rrohs sahl·bah·kheh*	wild rice
el asado *ehl ah·sah·doh*	roast
el atún *ehl ah·toon*	tuna
la avellana *lah ah·beh·yah·nah*	hazelnut
la avena *lah ah·beh·nah*	oatmeal
las aves *lahs ah·behs*	poultry
el azafrán *ehl ah·sah·frahn*	saffron
el azúcar *ehl ah·soo·kahr*	sugar
el bagre *ehl bah·greh*	catfish
la bebida *lah beh·bee·dah*	drink
el betabel *ehl beh·tah·behl*	beet
la berenjena *lah beh·rehn·kheh·nah*	eggplant [aubergine]
el nabo *ehl nah·boh*	parsnip
el berro *ehl beh·rroh*	watercress
el bollo *ehl boh·yoh*	bun
el brandy *ehl brahn·dee*	brandy
el brócoli *ehl broh·koh·lee*	broccoli
los brotes de bambú *lohs broh·tehs deh bahm·boo*	bamboo shoots

el buñuelo *ehl boo·nyweh·loh*	fritter
la cabra *lah kah·brah*	goat
el cabrito *ehl kah·bree·toh*	young goat
el cacahuate *ehl kah·kah·wah·teh*	peanut
el café *ehl kah·feh*	coffee
el café capuchino *ehl kah·feh kah·poo·chee·noh*	cappuccino
el café espresso *ehl kah·feh ehs·preh·soh*	espresso
la calabacita *lah kah·lah·bah·see·tah*	zucchini [courgette]
la calabaza *lah kah·lah·bah·sah*	pumpkin
el calamar *ehl kah·lah·mahr*	squid
el caldo *ehl kahl·doh*	broth
caldo tlalpeño *kahl·doh tlahl·peh·nyo*	soup made with vegetables, chicken and sometimes rice
los callos de hacha *lohs kah·yohs deh ah·chah*	scallop
el camarón *ehl kah·mah·rohn*	shrimp
el camote *lah kah·moh·teh*	yam
la canela *lah kah·neh·lah*	cinnamon
el cangrejo *ehl kahn·greh·khoh*	crab
el cangrejo gigante *ehl kahn·greh·khoh khee·gahn·teh*	spider crab
el caramelo *ehl kah·rah·meh·loh*	candy [sweet]
la carne asada *lah kahr·neh ah·sah·dah*	grilled meat
la carne *lah kahr·neh*	meat
la carne de cangrejo *lah kahr·neh deh kahn·greh·khoh*	crabmeat
la carne de puerco *lah kahr·neh deh pwehr·koh*	pork
la carne de res *lah kahr·neh deh rehs*	beef
la carne de venado *lah kahr·neh deh beh·nah·doh*	venison
la carne molida *lah kahr·neh moh·lee·dah*	ground beef
las carnes frías *lahs kahr·nehs free·ahs*	cold cuts [charcuterie]

el carnero *ehl kahr·neh·roh* — mutton
casero *kah·seh·roh* — homemade
la castaña *lah kahs·tah·nyah* — chestnut
el cazón *ehl kah·sohn* — baby shark
la cebolla *lah seh·boh·yah* — onion
el cebollín *elh seh·boh·yeen* — chives
la cebollita de rabo — scallion [spring onion]
lah seh·boh·yee·tah deh rrah·boh
la carne enlatada *lah kahr·neh ehn·lah·tah·dah* — corned beef
el centeno *ehl sehn·teh·noh* — rye
el cereal *ehl seh·reh·ahl* — cereal
la cereza *lah seh·reh·sah* — cherry
la cerveza *lah sehr·beh·sah* — beer
el cebollín *ehl seh·boh·yeen* — shallot
las chalupas *lahs chah·loo·pahs* — tortillas with potato, chicken, onion and salsa toppings

el champán *ehl chahm·pahn* — champagne
el champiñón *ehl chahm·pee·nyohn* — mushroom
el chícharo *ehl chee·chah·roh* — green pea
el chicharrón *ehl chee·chah·rrohn* — deep fried pork skin
el chile *ehl chee·leh* — hot pepper
el chile chipotle *ehl chee·leh chee·poh·tleh* — chipotle pepper
el chile jalapeño *ehl chee·leh khah·lah·peh·nyo* — jalapeño pepper
el chile piquín *ehl chee·leh pee·keen* — powdered red chili pepper
el chile relleno *ehl chee·leh reh·yeh·noh* — stuffed pepper
el chile verde *ehl chee·leh behr·deh* — green pepper
el nabo *ehl nah·boh* — parsnip
el chocolate *ehl choh·koh·lah·teh* — chocolate
el chocolate caliente — hot chocolate
ehl choh·koh·lah·teh kah·leeyehn·teh
la chuleta *lah choo·leh·tah* — chop

el acocil *ehl ah·koh·seel*	crayfish
el cilantro *ehl see·lahn·troh*	coriander
la ciruela *lah see·rweh·lah*	plum
la ciruela pasa *lah see·rweh·lah pah·sah*	prune
el clavo de olor *ehl klah·boh deh oh·lohr*	clove
el coco *ehl koh·koh*	coconut
la codorniz *lah koh·dohr·nees*	quail
la col *lah kohl*	cabbage
la col berza *lah kohl behr·sah*	kale
la col morada *lah kohl moh·rah·dah*	red cabbage
la cola de res *lah koh·lah deh rehs*	oxtail
las coles de Bruselas *lahs koh·lehs deh broo·seh·lahs*	Brussels sprouts
la coliflor *lah koh·lee·flohr*	cauliflower
el comino *ehl koh·mee·noh*	cumin
la compota *lah kohm·poh·tah*	stewed fruit
con alcohol *kohn ahl·kohl*	with alcohol
con crema *kohn kreh·mah*	with cream
la salsa de pepinillo *lah sahl·sah deh peh·pee·nee·yoh*	relish
el conejo *ehl koh·neh·khoh*	rabbit
el congrio *ehl kohn·greeyoh*	conger eel
los conos *lohs koh·nohs*	cone
las conservas *lahs kohnr·sehr·bahs*	pickled
el brandy *ehl brahn·dee*	brandy
el corazón *ehl koh·rah·sohn*	heart
el cordero *ehl kohr·deh·roh*	lamb
crema *creh·mah*	soup made with cream and assorted ingredients
la crema agria *lah kreh·mah ah·greeyah*	sour cream
la crema batida *lah kreh·mah bah·tee·dah*	whipped cream
crudo *kroo·doh*	raw

el cruasán *ehl croo•ah•sahn*	croissant
los dátiles *lohs dah•tee•lehs*	dates
descafeinado *dehs•kah•feh•ee•nah•doh*	decaffeinated
la dona *lah doh•nah*	doughnut
el durazno *ehl doo•rahs•noh*	peach
los ejotes *lohs eh•khoh•tehs*	green beans
la endivia *lah ehn•dee•beeyah*	endive
el endulzante artificial *ehl ehn•dool•sahn•teh ahr•tee•fee•seeyahl*	artificial sweetener
el eneldo *ehl eh•nehl•doh*	dill
la ensalada *lah ehn•sah•lah•dah*	salad
el espagueti *ehl ehs•pah•geh•tee*	spaghetti
la espaldilla *lah ehs•pahl•dee•yah*	shoulder
el espárrago *ehl ehs•pah•rrah•goh*	asparagus
las especias *lahs ehs•peh•seeyahs*	spices
la espinaca *lah ehs•pee•nah•kah*	spinach
el estragón *ehl ehs•trah•gohn*	tarragon
el faisán *ehl fahyee•sahn*	pheasant
la falda *lah fahl•dah*	beef brisket
el fideo *ehl fee•deh•oh*	noodle
el bistec *ehl bees•tehk*	steak
el flan *ehl flahn*	caramel custard
la fresa *lah freh•sah*	strawberry
los frijoles refritos *lohs free•khoh•lehs rreh•free•tohs*	mashed and fried black beans
la fruta *lah froo•tah*	fruit
las nueces *lahs nweh•sehs*	nuts
la galleta *lah gah•yeh•tah*	cookie [biscuit]
la galleta salada *lah gah•yeh•tah sah•lah•dah*	cracker
el ganso *ehl gahn•soh*	wild goose
el garbanzo *ehl gahr•bahn•soh*	chickpea

el germen de soya	bean sprouts
ehl khehr·mehnen· deh soh·yah	
la ginebra *lah khee·neh·brah*	gin
las gorditas *lahs gohr·dee·tahs*	little corn cakes baked or fried
la granada roja *lah grah·nah·dah roh·khah*	pomegranate
la granola *lah grah·noh·lah*	granola [muesli]
la grosella espinosa	gooseberry
lah groh·seh·yah ehs·pee·noh·sah	
la grosella negra *lah groh·seh·yah neh·grah*	black currant
la grosella roja *lah groh·seh·yah roh·khah*	red currant
el guacamole *ehl gwah·kah·moh·leh*	mashed avocado, onions, tomatoes and lime juice
la guayaba *lah gwah·yah·bah*	guava
la cereza agria *lah seh·reh·sah ah·grya geen·dah*	sour cherry
la hamburguesa *lah ahm·boor·geh·sah*	hamburger
la harina *lah ah·ree·nah*	flour
la harina de maíz *lah ah·ree·nah deh mah·ees*	cornmeal
el helado *ehl eh·lah·doh*	ice cream
el (cubito de) hielo	ice (cube)
ehl (kooh·bee·toh deh) eeyeh·loh	
el hígado *ehl ee·gah·doh*	liver
el higo *ehl ee·goh*	fig
el hinojo *ehl ee·noh·khoh*	fennel
la hoja de laurel *lah oh·khah deh lah·oo·rehl*	bay leaf
el hot dog *ehl khot dohg*	hot dog
el hueso *ehl weh·soh*	bone
el huevo *ehl weh·boh*	egg
el jabalí *ehl khah·bah·lee*	wild boar
la mermelada *lah mehr·meh·lah·dah*	jelly
el jamón *ehl khah·mohn*	ham
el jengibre *ehl khehn·khee·breh*	ginger

el jerez *ehl kheh·rehs*	sherry
el jitomate *ehl khee·toh·mah·teh*	tomato
el jocoque *ehl khoh·koh·keh*	buttermilk
el jugo *ehl khoo·goh*	juice
el kiwi *ehl kee·wee*	kiwi
la langosta *lah lahn·gohs·tah*	lobster
el langostino *ehl lahn·gohs·tee·noh*	prawn
la leche *lah leh·cheh*	milk
la leche de soya *lah leh·cheh deh soh·yah*	soymilk [soya milk]
el lechón *ehl leh·chohn*	suckling pig
la lechuga *lah leh·choo·gah*	lettuce
la lengua *lah lehn·gwah*	tongue
el lenguado *ehl lehn·gwah·doh*	sole
la lenteja *lah lehn·teh·khah*	lentil
el licor *ehl lee·kohr*	liqueur
el licor de naranja *ehl lee·kohr deh nah·rahn·khah*	orange liqueur
los licores *lohs lee·kohr·ehs*	spirits
la liebre *lah leeyeh·breh*	hare
el limón *ehl lee·mohn*	lime
el limón amarillo *ehl lee·mohn ah·mah·ree·yoh*	lemon
la limonada *lah leeh·moh·nah·dah*	lemonade
el lomo *ehl loh·moh*	loin
el robalo *el roo·bah·loh*	sea bass
los macarrones *lohs mah·kah·rroh·nehs*	macaroni
el maíz *ehl mah·ees*	sweet corn
la malteada *lah mahl·teh·ah·dah*	milk shake
la mandarina *lah mahn·dah·ree·nah*	tangerine
el mango *ehl mahn·goh*	mango
la mantequilla (con/sin sal)	butter (with/without salt)
lah mahn·teh·kee·yah (kohn/seen sahl)	
la margarina *lah mahr·gah·ree·nah*	margarine

la manzana	*lah mahn-sah-nah*	apple
la margarina	*lah mahr-gah-ree-nah*	margarine
el marisco	*ehl mah-rees-koh*	fish and shellfish
la mayonesa	*lah mah-yoh-neh-sah*	mayonnaise
el mazapán	*ehl mah-sah-pahn*	marzipan
el mejillón	*ehl meh-khee-yohn*	mussel
la mejorana	*lah meh-khoh-rah-nah*	marjoram
la melaza	*lah meh-lah-sah*	molasses
el melón	*ehl meh-lohn*	melon
la menta	*lah mehn-tah*	mint
las menudencias	*lahs meh-noo-dehn-seeyahs*	giblet
el merengue	*ehl meh-rehn-geh*	meringue
la merluza	*lah mehr-loo-sah*	hake
la mermelada	*lah mehr-meh-lah-dah*	marmalade/jam
el mero	*ehl meh-roh*	grouper
la miel	*lah meeyehl*	honey
el besugo	*ehl beh-soo-goh*	sea bream
la molleja	*lah moh-yeh-khah*	sweetbread
la morcilla	*lah mohr-see-yah*	black pudding
la mostaza	*lah mohs-tah-sah*	mustard
el nabo	*ehl nah-boh*	turnip
la naranja	*lah nah-rahn-khah*	orange
la natilla	*lah nah-tee-yah*	custard
el sorbete	*ehl sohr-beh-teh*	sorbet
la nuez	*lah nwehs*	pecan
la nuez moscada	*lah nwehs mohs-kah-dah*	nutmeg
el omelet	*ehl oh-meh-leht*	omelet
el Oporto	*ehl oh-pohr-toh*	port
el orégano	*ehl oh-reh-gah-noh*	oregano
el ostión	*ehl ohs-tyohn*	oyster
la paella	*lah pah-eh-yah*	rice dish

la paletilla *lah pah·leh·tee·yah*	shank
el palmito *ehl pahl·mee·toh*	palm heart
el pan *ehl pahn*	bread
el pan tostado *ehl pahn tohs·tah·doh*	toast
el panecillo *ehl pah·neh·see·yoh*	roll
la pancita *lah pahn·see·tah*	tripe
la papa *lah pah·pah*	potato
las papas fritas *lahs pah·pahs free·tahs*	French fries [chips], potato chips [crisps]
la papaya *lah pah·pah·yah*	papaya
la paprika *lah pah·pree·kah*	paprika
la pasa *lah pah·sah*	raisin
la pasta *lah pahs·tah*	pasta
la repostería *lah reh·pohs·teh·ree·ah*	pastry
el pastel *ehl pahs·tehl*	cake
la pata *lah pah·tah*	leg
las patas de puerco *lahs pah·tahs deh pwehr·koh*	pig's feet [trotters]
el paté *ehl pah·teh*	pâté
el pato *ehl pah·toh*	duck
el pato salvaje *ehl pah·toh sahl·bah·kheh*	wild duck
el pavo *ehl pah·boh*	turkey
la pechuga / filete (de pollo)	
la peh·choo·gah / fee·leh·teh (deh poh·yoh)	breast/ fillet (of chicken)
el pez sapo *ehl pehs ·sah·poh*	monkfish
el pepinillo *ehl peh·pee·nee·yoh*	pickle
el pepino *ehl peh·pee·noh*	cucumber
la pera *lah peh·rah*	pear
la perdiz *lah pehr·dees*	partridge
el perejil *ehl peh·reh·kheel*	parsley
el pescadito *ehl pehs·kah·dee·toh*	small fish
el pescado *ehl pehs·kah·doh*	fish

el pescado frito *ehl pehs·kah·doh free·toh* — fried fish

pescados y mariscos — seafood
pehs·kah·dohs ee mah·rees·kohs

el pez espada *ehl pes ehs·pah·dah* — swordfish

el pichón *ehl pee·chohn* — young pigeon

el pie *ehl pahee* — pie

el pie de queso *ehl pahee deh keh·soh* — cheesecake

pilsner *peelz·nehr* — pilsner (beer)

el pimentón dulce *ehl pee·mehn·tohn dool·seh* — paprika

la pimienta *lah pee·meeyehn·tah* — pepper (seasoning)

el pimiento rojo/verde ehl — red/green pepper
pee·meeyehn·toh roh·khoh/behr·deh

la pimienta negra — black pepper
lah pee·meeyehn·tah neh·grah

el pimiento *ehl pee·meeyehn·toh* — pepper (vegetable)

la piña *lah pee·nyah* — pineapple

los piñones *lohs pee·nyohn·ehs* — pine nuts

la pizza *lah peet·sah* — pizza

el plátano *ehl plah·tah·noh* — banana

el pollo *ehl poh·yoh* — chicken

el pollo frito *ehl poh·yoh free·toh* — fried chicken

el poro *ehl poh·roh* — leek

el pozole *ehl poh·soh·leh* — soup of stewed pork and corn kernels, garnished with lettuce, horseradish and oregano

el pulpo *ehl pool·poh* — octopus

las quesadillas *lahs keh·sah·dee·yahs* — corn tortillas stuffed with cheese, beef, chicken, etc.

el queso *ehl keh·soh* — cheese

el queso fundido *ehl keh·soh foon·dee·doh* — Mexican fondue

el rábano *ehl rrah·bah·noh*	radish
el raspado *ehl rrahs·pah·doh*	fruit flavored iced drink
los ravioles *lohs rrah·beeyoh·lehs*	ravioli
la raya *lah rrah·yah*	skate
el refresco *ehl rreh·frehs·koh*	soda
relleno *rreh·yeh·noh*	stuffed/stuffing
el requesón *ehl rreh·keh·sohn*	similar to ricotta cheese
la res *lah rrehs*	beef
el riñón *ehl rree·nyohn*	kidney
el romero *ehl rroh·meh·roh*	rosemary
el ron *ehl rrohn*	rum
rubia *rroo·beeyah*	lager (beer)
el ruibarbo *ehl rrooee·bahr·boh*	rhubarb
la sal *lah sahl*	salt
el salami *ehl sah·lah·mee*	salami
la salchicha *lah sahl·chee·chah*	sausage
el salmon *ehl sahl·mohn*	salmon
el salmonete *ehl sahl·moh·neh·teh*	red mullet
la salsa *lah sahl·sah*	chopped or pureed tomatoes, chiles, raw onions and cilantro
la salsa agridulce *lah sahl·sah ah·gree·dool·seh*	sweet and sour sauce
la salsa al mojo de ajo *lah sahl·sah ahl moh·khoh deh ah·kho*	garlic sauce
la salsa catsup *lah sahl·sah kaht·soop*	ketchup
la salsa de soya *lah sahl·sah deh soh·yah*	soy sauce
la salsa picante *lah sahl·sah pee·kahn·teh*	hot pepper sauce
la salvia *lah sahl·beeyah*	sage
la sandía *lah sahn·dee·ah*	watermelon
el sándwich *ehl sahnd·weech*	sandwich
la sangria *lah sahn·gree·ah*	wine punch
la sardina *lah sahr·dee·nah*	sardine

el sazonador *ehl sah·soh·nah·dohr*	allspice
la semilla *lah seh·mee·yah*	seed
la semilla de soya *lah seh·mee·yah deh soh·yah*	soybean [soyabean]
los sesos *lohs seh·sohs*	brains
la sidra *lah see·drah*	cider
el sirloin *ehl seer·loh·een*	sirloin
la sopa *lah soh·pah*	soup
sopa de lima *soh·pah deh lee·mah*	lima (citrus fruit) soup with seasoned chicken broth
sopa de tortilla *oh·pah deh tohr·tee·yah*	tomato broth garnished with fried tortilla strips, cream, avocado, cheese, chile and pork skin
la soya *lah soh·yah*	soy [soya]
el T-bone *ehl tee·bohn*	T-bone
los tacos *lohs tah·kohs*	soft tortillas filled with a variety of meat and vegetables
el té *ehl teh*	tea
la ternera *lah tehr·neh·rah*	veal
el tequila *ehl teh·kee·lah*	tequila
el tiburón *ehl tee·boo·rohn*	shark
tinto *teen·toh*	red (wine)
el tocino *ehl toh·see·noh*	bacon
el tomillo *ehl toh·mee·yoh*	thyme
la toronja *lah toh·rohn·khah*	grapefruit
la tortilla *lah tohr·tee·yah*	thin, flat bread made of corn
el trigo *ehl tree·goh*	wheat
las tripas *lahs tree·pahs*	organ meat [offal]
la trucha *lah troo·chah*	trout
las trufas *lahs troo·fahs*	truffles
la verdura *lah behr·doo·rah*	vegetable
la zanahoria *lah sah·nah·oh·reeyah*	carrot

People

Conversation   99

Romance   105

Conversation

ESSENTIAL

Hello!/Hi!	**¡Hola!** *oh·lah*
How are you?	**¿Cómo estás?** *koh·moh ehs·tahs*
Fine, thanks.	**Bien, gracias.** *beeyehn grah·seeyahs*
Excuse me!	**¡Disculpe!** *dihs·koohl·peh*
Do you speak English?	**¿Habla inglés?** *ah·blah een·glehs*
What's your name?	**¿Cómo se llama?** *koh·moh seh yah·màh*
My name is…	**Me llamo…** *meh yah·moh…*
Nice to meet you.	**Encantado** *m* /**Encantada** *f*.
	ehn·kahn·tah·doh /ehn·kahn·tah·dah
Where are you from?	**¿De dónde es usted?**
	deh dohn·deh es oos·tehd
I'm from the U.K./U.S.	**Soy de Estados Unidos/del Reino Unido.**
	soy deh ehs·tah·dohs oo·nee·dohs/dehl rreyee·noh
	oo·nee·doh
What do you do for a living?	**¿A qué se dedica?**
	ah keh seh deh·dee·kah
I work for…	**Trabajo para…**
	trah·bah·khoh pah·rah…
I'm a student.	**Soy estudiante.**
	soy ehs·too·deeyahn·teh
I'm retired.	**Estoy jubilado** *m* /**jubilada** *f*.
	ehs·toy khoo·bee·lah·doh /khoo·bee·lah·dah
Do you like…?	**¿Le gusta…?** *leh goos·tah…*
Goodbye.	**Adiós.** *ah·deeyohs*
See you later.	**Hasta luego.** *ah·stah lweh·goh*

In Mexican Spanish, there are a number of forms for 'you' taking different verb forms: **tú** (singular, informal), **usted** (singular, formal) and **ustedes** (plural). When addressing strangers, always use the more formal **usted** (singular) as opposed to the more familiar **tú** (singular), until told otherwise. If you know someone's professional title, it's polite to use it, e.g., **doctor** (male doctor), **doctora** (female doctor). You can also simply say **Señor** (Mr.), **Señora** (Mrs.) or **Señorita** (Miss).

Language Difficulties

Do you speak English?	**¿Habla inglés?** *ah·blah een·glehs*
Does anyone here speak English?	**¿Hay alguien aquí que hable inglés?** *aye ahl·geeyen ah·kee keh ah·bleh een·glehs*
I don't speak (much) Spanish.	**No hablo (mucho) español.** *noh ah·bloh(moo·choh) ehs·pah·nyol*
Can you speak more slowly?	**¿Puede hablar más despacio?** *pweh·deh ah·blahr mahs dehs·pah·seeyoh*
Can you repeat that?	**¿Podría repetir eso?** *poh·dree·ah rreh·peh·teer eh·soh*
Excuse me?	**¿Cómo?** *koh·moh*
Can you spell it?	**¿Lo puede deletrear?** *loh pweh·deh deh·leh·treh·ahr*
Please write it down.	**Escríbamelo, por favor.** *ehs·kree·bah·meh·loh pohr fah·bohr*
Can you translate this into English for me?	**¿Podría traducirme esto al inglés?** *poh·dree·ah trah·doo·seer·meh ehs·toh ahl een·glehs*
What does this/ that mean?	**¿Qué significa esto/eso?** *keh seeg·nee·fee·kah ehs·toh/eh·soh*
I understand.	**Entiendo.** *ehn·teeyehn·doh*
I don't understand.	**No entiendo.** *noh ehn·teeyehn·doh*
Do you understand?	**¿Entiende?** *ehn·teeyehn·deh*

YOU MAY HEAR...

Hablo muy poco inglés.
ah•bloh mooy poh•koh een•glehs

No hablo inglés
ah•bloh een•glehs

I only speak a little
English.
I don't speak English.

Making Friends

Hello!	**¡Hola!** *oh•lah*
Good afternoon.	**Buenas tardes.** *bweh•nahs tahr•dehs*
Good evening.	**Buenas noches.** *bweh•nahs noh•chehs*
My name is...	**Me llamo...** *meh yah•moh...*
What's your name?	**¿Cómo te llamas?** *koh•moh teh yah•mahs*
I'd like to introduce you to...	**Quiero presentarle a...** *keeyeh•roh preh•sehn•tahr•leh ah...*
Pleased to meet you.	**Encantado** *m* /**Encantada** *f* . *ehn•kahn•tah•doh/ehn•kahn•tah•dah*
How are you?	**¿Cómo estás?** *koh•moh ehs•tahs*
Fine, thanks. And you?	**Bien gracias. ¿Y usted?** *beeyehn grah•seeyahs ee oos•tehd*

When meeting someone for the first time in Mexico greet him or her with **hola** (hello), **buenos días** (good morning), **buenas tardes** (good afternoon) or **buenas noches** (good evening). Mexicans even extend this general greeting to strangers when in elevators, waiting rooms and other small public spaces. A general acknowledgment or reply is expected from all. When leaving, say **adiós** (goodbye).

Travel Talk

I'm here...	**Estoy aquí...**	*ehs·toy ah·kee...*
on business	**en viaje de negocios**	
	ehn beeyah·kheh deh neh·goh·seeyohs	
on vacation [holiday]	**de vacaciones** *deh bah·kah·seeyoh·nehs*	
studying	**estudiando** *ehs·too·deeyahn·doh*	
I'm staying for...	**Voy a quedarme...** *boy ah keh·dahr·meh...*	
I've been here...	**Llevo aquí...** *yeh·boh ah·kee...*	
a day	**un día** *oon dee·ah*	
a week	**una semana** *oo·nah seh·mah·nah*	
a month	**un mes** *oon mehs*	
Where are you from?	**¿De dónde es usted?** *deh dohn·deh ehs oos·tehd*	
I'm from...	**Soy de...** *soy deh...*	

For Numbers, see page 167.

Personal

Who are you with?	**¿Con quién vino?** *kohn keeyehn beeh·noh*	
I'm here alone.	**Vine solo** *m* **/sola** *f.* *beeh·neh soh·loh/soh·lah*	
I'm with...	**Vine con mi...** *beeh·neh kohn mee...*	
my husband/wife	**esposo** *m* **/esposa** *f* *ehs·poh·soh /ehs·poh·sah*	
my boyfriend/	**novio** *m* **/novia** *f*	
girlfriend	*noh·beeyoh /noh·beeyah*	

a friend/friends/a colleague/ colleagues	**amigo(s)/colega(s)** *ah·mee·goh(s)/koh·leh·gah(s)*
When's your birthday?	**¿Cuándo es su cumpleaños?** *kwahn·doh ehs soo koom·pleh·ah·nyohs*
How old are you?	**¿Cuántos años tiene?** *kwahntohs ahn·yos teeyeh·neh*
I'm…	**Tengo…años.** *tehn·goh… ah·nyohs*
Are you married?	**¿Está casado** *m* **/casada** *f* **?** *ehs·tah kah·sah·doh /kah·sah·dah*
I'm…	**Estoy…** *ehs·toy…*
single/in a relationship	**soltero** *m* **/soltera** *f sohl·teh·roh /sohl·teh·rah/* **en una relación** *ehn oo·nah rreh·lah·seeyohn*
engaged	**comprometido** *m* **comprometida** *f kom·pro·meh·tee·doh/com·pro·meh·tee·dah*
married	**casado** *m* **/casada** *f kah·sah·doh/kah·sah·dah*
divorced	**divorciado** *m* **/divorciada** *f dee·bohr·seeyah·doh /dee·bohr·seeyah·dah*
separated	**separado** *m* **/separada** *f seh·pah·rah·doh /seh·pah·rah·dah*
widowed	**Soy viudo** *m* **/viuda** *f* **.** *soy beeyoo·doh/ beeyoo·dah*
Do you have children / grandchildren ?	**¿Tiene hijos/nietos?** *teeyeh·neh ee·khohs/neeyeh·tohs*

Work & School

What do you do for a living?	**¿A qué se dedica?** *ah keh sehdeh·dee·kah*
What are you studying?	**¿Qué estudia?** *keh ehs·too·deeyah*
I'm studying Spanish.	**Estudio español.** *ehs·too·deeyoh ehs·pah·nyohl*

I…	**Yo…** *yoh…*
work full-/ part-time	**trabajo tiempo completo/medio tiempo** *trah·bah·khoh teeyehm·poh kohm·pleh·toh/meh·deeoh teeyehm·poh*
am unemployed	**estoy desempleado** *ehs·toy dehs·ehm·pleh·ah·doh*
work at home	**trabajo desde casa** *trah·bah·khoh sdehz·deh kah·sah*
Who do you work for?	**¿Para quién trabaja?** *pah·rah keeyehn trah·bah·khah*
I work for…	**Trabajo para…** *trah·bah·khoh pah·rah…*
Here's my business card.	**Aquí tiene mi tarjeta.** *ah·kee teeyeh·neh mee tahr·kheh·tah*

For Business Travel, see page 141.

Weather

What's the forecast?	**¿Cuál es el pronóstico del tiempo?** *kwahl ehs ehl proh·nohs·tee·koh dehl teeyehm·poh*
What beautiful/ terrible weather!	**¡Qué clima más bonito/feo hace!** *keh clee·mah mahs boh·nee·toh/feh·oh ah·seh*
It's…	
cool/warm	**Hace frío/calor.** *ah·seh free·oh/kah·lohr*
cold/hot	**frío/caliente** *free·oh/cah·lyehn·teh*
rainy/sunny	**Está llvioso/soleado.** *ehs·tah yoo·beeyoh·soh/soh·leh·ah·doh*
snowy/icy	**Hay nieve/hielo.** *aye neeyeh·beh/eeyeh·loh*
Do I need a jacket/ an umbrella?	**¿Necesito una chamarra/un paraguas?** *neh·seh·see·toh oo·nah chah·mah·rrah/ oon pah·rah·gwahs*

For Temperature, see page 172.

ESSENTIAL

Would you like to go out for a drink/dinner?	**¿Le gustaría salir a tomar una copa/cenar?** *leh goos•tah•ree•ah sah•leer ah toh•mahr oo•nah koh•pah/seh•nahr*
What are your plans for tonight/ tomorrow?	**¿Qué planes tiene para esta noche/ mañana?** *keh plah•nehs teeyeh•neh pah•rah ehs•tah noh•cheh/ mah•nyah•nah*
Can I have your (phone) number?	**¿Puede darme su número?** *pweh•deh dahr•meh soo noo•meh•roh*
Can I join you?	**¿Puedo acompañarlo m /acompañarla f?** *pweh•doh ah•kohm•pah•nyahr•loh / ah•kohm•pah•nyahr•lah*
Can I buy you a drink?	**¿Puedo invitarle una copa?** *pweh•doh een•bee•tahr•leh oo•nah koh•pah*
I love you.	**Te amo.** *teh ah•moh*

The Dating Game

Would you like to go out...?	**¿Te gustaría salir a...?** *Teh goos•tah•ree•ah sah•leer ah...*
for coffee	**tomar un café** *toh•mahr oon kah•feh*
for a drink	**tomar una copa** *toh•mahr oona koh•pah*
to dinner	**cenar** *seh•nahr*
What are your plans for...?	**¿Qué vas a hacer...?** *keh bahs ah ah•sehr...*
today	**hoy** *oy*
tonight	**esta noche** *ehs•tah noh•cheh*

tomorrow	**mañana** *mah•nyah•nah*
this weekend	**este fin de semana**
	ehs•teh feen deh seh•mah•nah
Where would you like to go?	**¿Adónde te gustaría ir?**
	ah•dohn•deh teh goos•tah•ree•ah eer
I'd like to go to…	**Me gustaría ir a…**
	meh goos•tah•ree•ah eer ah…
Do you like…?	**¿Te gusta…?** *Teh goos•tah…*
Can I have your phone number/ e-mail?	**¿Puedes darme tu número/dirección de correo electrónico?** *pweh•dehs dahr•meh too noo•meh•roh/ dee•rehk•seeyohn deh koh•rreh•oh eh•lehk•troh•nee•koh*
Are you on Facebook /Twitter?	**¿Estás en Facebook o Twitter?**
	ehs•tahs ehn Facebook o Twitter
Can I join you?	**¿Puedo acompañarte?**
	pweh•doh ah•kohm•pah•nyahr•teh
You're very attractive.	**Eres muy guapo** *m* /**guapa** *f.*
	Ehrehs mooy gwah•poh/gwah•pah
Let's go somewhere quieter.	**Vayamos a un sitio más tranquilo.**
	bah•yah•mohs ah oon see•teeyoh mahs trahn•kee•loh

For Communications, see page 48.

Accepting & Rejecting

I'd love to.	**Me encantaría.**
	meh ehn•kahn•tah•ree•yah
Where should we meet?	**¿Dónde nos vemos?**
	dohn•deh nohs beh•mohs
I'll meet you at the bar/your hotel.	**Nos vemos en el bar/tu hotel.**
	nohs beh•mohs ehn ehl bahr/too oh•tehl
I'll come by at…	**Pasaré a…**
	pah•sah•reh ah…

I'm busy.	**Estoy ocupado *m* /ocupada *f*.**
	ehs•toy oh•koo•pah•doh/oh•koo•pah•dah
I'm not interested.	**No me interesa.** *noh meh een•teh•reh•sah*
Leave me alone.	**Déjeme en paz.** *deh•kheh•meh ehn pahs*
Stop bothering me!	**¡Deje de molestarme!**
	deh•kheh deh moh•lehs•tahr•meh

For Time, see page 169.

Getting Intimate

Can I hug/kiss you?	**¿Puedo abrazarte/besarte?**
	pweh•doh ah•brah•sahr•teh/beh•sahr•teh
Yes.	**Sí.** *see*
No.	**No.** *noh*
Stop!	**¡Basta!** *bahs•tah*
I love you.	**Te amo.** *teh ah•moh*

Sexual Preferences

Are you gay?	**¿Eres gay?** *erehs gay*
I'm...	**Soy...** *soy...*
heterosexual	**heterosexual** *eh•teh•roh•sex•wahl*
homosexual	**homosexual** *oh•moh•sex•wahl*
bisexual	**bisexual** *bee•sex•wahl*
Do you like men/women?	**¿Te gustan los hombres/las mujeres?**
	Teh goos•tahn lohs ohm•brehs/lahs moo•kheh•rehs pi-daet-kur miay-his-tae/nahi-sis-tah

Leisure Time

Sightseeing 109
Shopping 114
Sport & Leisure 131
Going Out 137

LA MARINA

Sightseeing

ESSENTIAL

Where's the tourist information office?	**¿Dónde está la oficina de turismo?** *dohn•deh ehs•tah lah oh•fee•see•nah deh too•reez•moh*
What are the main sights?	**¿Dónde están los principales sitios de interés?** *dohn•deh ehs•tahn lohs preen•see•pah•lehs see•teeyohs deh een•teh•rehs*
Do you offer tours in English?	**¿Hay recorridos en inglés?** *aye rreh•koh•rree•dohs ehn een•glehs*
Can I have a map/ guide?	**¿Puede darme un mapa/una guía?** *pweh•deh dahr•meh oon mah•pah/oo•nah gee•ah*

Tourist Information

Do you have information on...?	**¿Tiene información sobre...?** *teeyeh•neh een•fohr•mah•seeyohn soh•breh...*
Can you recommend...?	**¿Puede recomendarme...?** *pweh•deh rreh•koh•mehn•dahr•meh...*
a bus tour	**un paseo en camión** *oon pah•seh•oh ehn kah•meeyohn*
an excursion to...	**una excursión a...** *oo•nah ehx•koor•seeyohn ah...*
a tour of...	**un paseo de...** *oon pah•seh•oh deh*

Tourist offices can be found in major Mexican cities and in many of the smaller towns popular with tourists. They generally work regular business hours Monday to Friday and work shorter days on Saturdays and Sundays. Information can also be found via the Mexican Tourism Board's official website www.visitmexico.com.

On Tour

I'd like to go on the excursion to…	**Quiero ir en la excursión a…** *keeyeh·roh eer ehn lah hehx·koor·seeohn ah…*
When's the next tour?	**¿Cuándo es el próximo recorrido?** *kwahn·doh ehs ehl proh·xee·moh rreh·koh·rree·doh*
Are there tours in English?	**¿Hay paseos en inglés?** *aye pah·seh·ohs ehn een·glehs*
Is there an English guide book/audio guide?	**¿Hay una guía/audioguía en inglés?** *aye oo·nah gee·ah/awoo·deeyoh·gee·ah ehn een·glehs*
What time do we leave/return?	**¿A qué hora salimos/regresamos?** *ah keh oh·rah sah·lee·mohs/rreh·greh·sah·mohs*
We'd like to see…	**Queremos ver…** *keh·reh·mohs behr…*
Can we stop here…?	**¿Podemos parar aquí…?** *poh·deh·mohs pah·rahr ah·kee…*
to take photos	**para tomar fotos** *pah·rah toh·mahr foh·tohs*
for souvenirs	**para comprar recuerdos** *pah·rah kohm·prahr rreh·kwehr·dohs*
for the toilets	**para ir al baño** *pah·rah eer ahl bah·nyo*

Is it disabled-accessible?	**¿Tiene acceso para discapacitados?**
	teeyeh·neh ahk·seh·soh pah·rah
	dees·kah·pah·see·tah·dohs

For Tickets, see page 19.

Seeing the Sights

Where's…?	**¿Dónde está/están…?**
	dohn·deh ehs·tah/ehs·tahn…
the battleground	**el campo de batalla**
	ehl kahm·poh deh bah·tah·yah
the botanical garden	**el jardín botánico**
	ehl khahr·deen boh·tah·nee·koh
the castle	**el castillo** *ehl kahs·tee·yoh*
the downtown	**el centro** *ehl sehn·troh*
the fountain	**la fuente** *lah fwehn·teh*
the library	**la biblioteca** *lah bee·bleeyoh·teh·kah*
the market	**el mercado** *ehl mehr·kah·doh*
the museum	**el museo** *ehl moo·seh·oh*
the old town	**el centro histórico** *ehl sehn·troh ees·toh·reekoh*
the opera house	**la ópera …** *lah oh·peh·rah*
the palace	**el palacio** *ehl pah·lah·seeyoh*

the park	**el parque** *ehl pahr•keh*
the ruins	**las ruinas** *lahs rrwee•nahs*
the shopping area	**la zona comercial** *lahs soh•nah koh•mehr•seeyahl*
the town square	**la plaza** *lah plah•sah*
Can you show me	**¿Puede enseñármelo en el mapa?**
on the map?	*pweh•deh ehn•seh•nyahr•meh•loh ehn ehl mah•pah*
It's...	**Es...** *ehs...*
amazing	**increíble** *een•kreh•ee•bleh*
beautiful	**precioso** *preh•seeyoh•soh*
boring	**aburrido** *ah•boo•rree•doh*
interesting	**interesante** *een•teh•reh•sahn•teh*
magnificent	**magnífico** *mahg•nee•fee•koh*
romantic	**romántico** *rroh•mahn•tee•koh*
strange	**raro** *rrah•roh*
terrible	**horrible** *oh•rree•bleh*
ugly	**feo** *feh•oh*
I (don't) like it.	**(No) Me gusta.** *(noh) meh goo•stah*

For Asking Directions, see page 33.

Religious Sites

Where's…?	**¿Dónde está…?**
	dohn•deh ehs•tah…
the cathedral	**la catedral**
	lah kah•teh•drahl
the Catholic/	**la iglesia católica/protestante**
Protestant church	*lah ee•gleh•seeyah kah•toh•lee•kah/*
	proh•tehs•tahn•teh
the mosque	**la mezquita**
	lah mehs•kee•tah
the shrine	**el santuario**
	ehl sahn•twah•reeyoh
the synagogue	**la sinagoga**
	lah see•nah•goh•gah
the temple	**el templo**
	ehl tehm•ploh
What time is mass/	**¿A qué hora es la misa/el servicio?**
the service?	*ah keh oh•rah ehs lah mee•sah/ehl sehr•bee•seeyoh*

Shopping

ESSENTIAL

Where's the market/ mall?	**¿Dónde está el mercado/centro comercial?** *dohn•deh ehs•tah ehl mehr•kah•doh/sen•troh koh•mehr•seeyahl*
I'm just looking.	**Sólo estoy mirando.** *soh•loh ehs•toy mee•rahn•doh*
Can you help me?	**¿Puede ayudarme?** *pweh•deh ah•yoo•dahr•meh*
I'm being helped.	**Ya me atienden.** *yah meh ah•teeyehn•dehn*
How much?	**¿Cuánto es?** *kwahn•toh ehs*
That one, please.	**Ése** *m* **/Ésa** *f* **, por favor.** *eh•seh /eh•sah pohr fah•bohr*
That's all.	**Eso es todo.** *eh•soh ehs toh•doh*
Where can I pay?	**¿Dónde se paga?** *dohn•deh seh pah•gah*
I'll pay in cash/by credit card.	**Voy a pagar en efectivo/con tarjeta de crédito.** *boy ah pah•gahr ehn eh•fehk•tee•boh/ kohn tahr•kheh•tah deh kreh•dee•toh*
A receipt, please.	**Un comprobante, por favor.** *oon kohm•proh•bahn•teh pohr fah•bohr*

At the Shops

Where's...?	**¿Dónde está/están...?** *dohn•deh ehs•tah/ehs•tahn...*
the antiques store	**la tienda de antigüedades** *lah teeyehn•dah deh ahn•tee•gweh•dah•dehs*
the bakery	**la panadería** *lah pah•nah•deh•ree•ah*
the bank	**el banco** *ehl bahn•koh*
the bookstore	**la librería** *lah lee•breh•ree•ah*
the clothing store	**la tienda de ropa** *lah teeyehn•dah deh rroh•pah*

the delicatessen	**la salchichonería** *lah sahl·chee·choh·neh·ree·ah*
the department store	**las tiendas departamentales** *lahs teeyehn·dahs deh·pahr·tah·mehn·tah·lehs*
the gift shop	**la tienda de regalos** *lah teeyehn·dah deh rreh·gah·lohs*
the health food store	**la tienda de alimentos naturales** *lah teeyehn·dah deh ah·lee·mehn·tohs nah·too·rahl·ehs*
the jeweler	**la joyería** *lah khoh·yeh·ree·ah*
the liquor store [off-licence]	**la licorería** *lah lee·coh·reh·ree·ah*
the market	**el mercado** *ehl mehr·kah·doh*
the music store	**la tienda de música** *lah teey-ehn·dah deh moo·see·kah*
the pastry shop	**la pastelería** *lah pahs·teh·leh·ree·ah*
the pharmacy	**la farmacia** *lah fahr·mah·seeyah*
the produce [grocery] store	**la tienda de frutas y verduras** *lah teeyehn·dah deh froo·tahs ee behr·doo·rahs*
the shoe store	**la zapatería** *lah sah·pah·teh·ree·ah*
the shopping mall	**el centro comercial** *ehl sehn·troh koh·mehr·seeyahl*
the souvenir store	**la tienda de recuerdos** *lah teeyehn·dah deh rreh·kwehr·dohs*

the supermarket	**el supermercado** *ehl soo•pehr•mehr•kah•doh*
the tobacconist	**la tabaquería** *lah tah•bah•keh•ree•ah*
the toy store	**la juguetería** *lah khoo•geh•teh•ree•ah*

Ask an Assistant

When do you open/close?	**¿A qué hora abren/cierran?** *ah keh oh•rah ah•brehn/seeyeh•rrahn*
the cashier	**la caja** *lah kah•khah*
the escalator	**las escaleras eléctricas** *lahs ehs•kah•leh•rahs eh•lehk•tree•kahs*
the elevator [lift]	**el elevador** *ehl eh•leh•bah•dohr*
the fitting room	**el probador** *ehl proh•bah•dohr*
the store directory	**la guía de tiendas** *lah gee•ah deh teeyehn•dahs*
Can you help me?	**¿Puede ayudarme?** *pweh•deh ah•yoo•dahr•meh*
I'm just looking.	**Sólo estoy mirando.** *soh•loh ehs•toy mee•rahn•doh*
I'm being helped.	**Ya me atienden.** *yah meh ah•teeyehn•dehn*
Do you have…?	**¿Tienen…?** *teeyeh•nehn…*
Can you show me…?	**¿Podría enseñarme…?** *poh•dree•ah ehn•seh•nyahr•meh…*
Can you ship/wrap it?	**¿Pueden hacer un envío/envolverlo?** *pweh•dehn ah•sehr oon ehn•bee•oh/ehn•bohl•behr•loh*
How much?	**¿Cuánto es?** *kwahn•toh ehs*
That's all.	**Eso es todo.** *eh•soh ehs toh•doh*

For Souvenirs, see page 129.

YOU MAY HEAR…

¿Necesita ayuda? *neh•seh•see•tah ah•yoo•dah*	Can I help you?
Un momento. *oon moh•mehn•toh*	One moment.
¿Qué desea? *keh deh•seh•ah*	What would you like?
¿Algo más? *ahl•goh mahs*	Anything else?

YOU MAY SEE...

ABIERTO/CERRADO	open/closed
CERRADO DURANTE EL ALMUERZO	closed for lunch
PROBADOR	fitting room
CAJERO	cashier
SOLO EFECTIVO	cash only
SE ACEPTAN TARJETAS DE CRÉDITO	credit cards accepted
HORARIO DE ATENCIÓN	business hours
SALIDA	exit

Personal Preferences

I'd like something...	**Quiero algo...**
	keeyeh•roh ahl•goh...
cheap/expensive	**barato/caro** *bah•rah•toh/kah•roh*
larger/smaller	**más grande/más pequeño**
	mahs grahn•deh/mahs peh•keh•nyoh
from this region	**de esta región** *deh ehs•tah rreh•kheeyohn*
Around...pesos.	**De unos...pesos.** *deh oo•nohs...peh•sohs*
Is it real?	**¿Es auténtico** *m* **/auténtica** *f***?**
	ehs awoo•tehn•tee•koh/awoo•tehn•tee•kah

Can you show me this/that ?	**¿Puede mostrarme esto/eso?**
	pweh·deh mohs·trahr·meh ehs·toh/eh·soh
That's not quite what I want.	**Eso no es realmente lo que busco.**
	eh·soh noh ehs rreh·ahl·mehn·teh loh keh boos·koh
No, I don't like it.	**No, no me gusta.** *noh noh meh goos·tah*
It's too expensive.	**Es demasiado caro.**
	ehs deh·mah·seeyah·doh kah·roh
I have to think about it.	**Voy a pensarlo.** *boy ah pehn·sahr·loh*
I'll take it.	**Me lo llevo.** *meh loh yeh·boh*

Paying & Bargaining

How much?	**¿Cuánto es?** *kwahn·toh ehs*
I'll pay…	**Voy a pagar…** *boy ah pah·gahr…*
in cash	**en efectivo** *ehn eh·fehk·tee·boh*
by credit card	**con tarjeta de crédito**
	kohn tahr·kheh·tah deh kreh·dee·toh
by traveller's cheque	**con cheque de viajero**
	kohn cheh·keh deh beeyah·kheh·roh
A receipt, please.	**Un comprobante, por favor.**
	oon kohm·proh·bahn·teh pohr fah·bohr
That's too much.	**Eso es mucho.** *eh·soh ehs moo·choh*
I'll give you…	**Le doy…** *leh doy…*
I have only…pesos.	**Sólo tengo…pesos.** *soh·loh tehn·goh…peh·sohs*
Is that your best price?	**¿Es el mejor precio que me puede dar?**
	ehs ehl meh·khohr preh·seeyoh keh meh pweh·deh dahr
Can you give me a discount?	**¿En cuánto me lo deja?**
	ehn kwahn·toh meh loh deh·khah

For Numbers, see page 167.

Tarjetas de crédito (credit cards) are widely accepted, although you may be asked to show ID when using one. **Tarjetas de débito** (debit cards) are also common. Traveler's checks are not accepted everywhere; have an alternative form of payment available. Cash is the preferred method of payment—some places, such as chain convenience stores, newsstands, tobacconists, flower shops and market or street vendors will only take cash. **Mercados** (markets) and **mercados sobre ruedas** (traveling markets) are popular. A wide variety of goods is available at these markets, including fruit and vegetables, antiques, souvenirs, regional items and so on. Your hotel or local tourist office will have information on the markets in your area. Most **mercados** are open daily from early morning until late afternoon; the **mercados sobre ruedas** times vary by location.

YOU MAY HEAR...

¿Cómo va a pagar? koh·moh bah ah pah·gahr — How are you paying?

Rechazaron su tarjeta. — Your card has been
rreh·chah·sah·rohn soo tahr·kheh·tah — declined.

Su identificación, por favor. — ID please.
soo ee·dehn·tee·fee·kah·seeyohn pohr fah·bohr

No aceptamos tarjetas de crédito. — We don't accept credit
noh ah·sehp·tah·mohs tahr·kheh·tahs — cards.
deh kreh·dee·toh

Sólo en efectivo, por favor. — Cash only, please.
soh·loh ehn eh·fehk·tee·boh pohr fah·bohr

Making a Complaint

I'd like...	**Quiero...** *keeyeh·roh...*
to exchange this	**cambiar esto por otro**
	kahm·beeyahr ehs·toh pohr oh·troh
a refund	**que me devuelvan el dinero**
	keh meh deh·bwehl·bahn ehl dee·neh·roh
to see the manager	**hablar con el encargado**
	ah·blahr kohn ehl ehn·kahr·gah·doh

Services

Can you recommend...?	**¿Puede recomendarme...?** *pweh·deh rreh·koh·mehn·dahr·meh...*
a barber	**una peluquería** *oo·nah peh·loo·keh·ree·ah*
a dry cleaner	**una tintorería** *oo·nah teen·toh·reh·ree·ah*
a hairstylist	**un salón de belleza** *oon sah·lohn deh beh·yeh·sah*
a Laundromat [launderette]	**una lavandería** *oo·nah lah·bahn·deh·ree·ah*
a nail salon	**el manicurista** *ehl mah·nee·koo·rees·tah*
a spa	**spa** *ehs·pah*
a travel agency	**una agencia de viajes**
	oo·nah ah·hehn·seeah deh bee-ah·hehs
Can you...this?	**¿Puede...esto?** *pweh·deh...ehs·toh*
alter	**hacerle un arreglo a** *ah·sehr·leh oon ah·rreh·gloh ah*
clean	**limpiar** *leem·peeyahr*
fix	**zurcir** *soor·seer*
press	**planchar** *plahn·chahr*
When will it be ready?	**¿Cuándo estará listo?** *kwahn·doh ehs·tah·rah lees·toh*

Hair & Beauty

I'd like...	**Quiero...** *keeyeh·roh...*
an appointment for today/tomorrow	**hacer cita para hoy/mañana** *ah·sehr see·tah pah·rah oy/mah·nyah·nah*

some color/	**pintarme el pelo**
highlights	*peen·tahr·meh ehl peh·loh*
my hair styled/	**un peinado/que me sequen el pelo**
blow-dried	*oon peh-ee·nah·doh/keh meh seh·kehn ehl peh·loh*
a haircut	**cortarme el pelo** *kohr·tahr·meh ehl peh·loh*
an eyebrow/	**depilarme las cejas/ingles**
bikini wax	*deh·pee·lahr·meh lahs seh·khahs/een·glehs*
a facial	**hacerme un facial** *ah·sehr·meh oon fah·seeyahl*
a manicure/	**hacerme el manicure/pedicure**
pedicure	*ah·sehr·meh ehl mah·nee·koo·reh/peh·dee·koo·reh*
a (sports) massage	**un masaje (deportivo)**
	oon mah·sah·kheh (deh·pohr·tee·boh)
A trim, please.	**cortarme las puntas** *kohr·tahr·meh lahs poon·tahs*
Not too short.	**No me lo corte demasiado.**
	noh meh loh kohr·teh deh·mah·seeyah·doh
Shorter here.	**Quíteme más de aquí.** *kee·teh·meh mahs deh ah·kee*
Do you offer…?	**¿Hacen…?** *ah·sehn…*
acupuncture	**acupuntura** *ah·koo·poon·too·rah*
aromatherapy	**aromaterapia** *ah·roh·mah·teh·rah·peeyah*
oxygen	**oxígenoterapia** *oh·xee·kheh·noh·teh·rah·peeyah*
a sauna	**¿Tienen un sauna?** *teeyeh·nehn oon sawoo·nah*

Mexico has many **spas, wellness centers** and **health-based resorts.** These facilities offer a wide selection of treatments, including relaxation therapies and herbal remedies. Resort and overnight spas often offer individual services to those not staying there. Many of these also offer other leisure activities such as horseback riding, guided tours, golf and swimming. Some spas and resorts do not allow children, so check before booking if you are traveling with kids.

Antiques

How old is it?	**¿Qué antigüedad tiene?** *keh ahn·tee·gweh·dahd teeyeh·neh*
Do you have anything from the…period?	**¿Tiene algo de la época…?** *teeyeh·neh ahl·goh deh lah eh·poh·kah…*
Do I have to fill out any forms?	**¿Tengo que llenar algún formulario?** *tehn·goh keh yeh·nahr ahl·goon fohr·moo·lah·reeoh*
Is there a certificate of authenticity?	**¿Tiene el certificado de autenticidad?** *teeyeh·neh ehl sehr·tee·fee·kah·doh deh awoo·tehn·tee·see·dahd*
Can you ship/ wrap it?	**¿Pueden hacer un envío/envolverlo?** *pweh·dehn ah·sehr oon ehn·bee·oh/ehn·bohl·behr·loh*

Clothing

I'd like…	**Quiero…** *keeyeh·roh…*
Can I try this on?	**¿Puedo probarme esto?** *pweh·doh proh·bahr·meh ehs·toh*
It doesn't fit.	**No me queda bien.** *noh meh keh·dah beeyehn*
It's too…	**Me queda demasiado…** *meh keh·dah deh·mah·seeyah·doh…*
big/small	**grande** *grahn·deh*/ **chico** *m*/**chica** *f chee·koh /chee·kah*

short/long	**corto m /corta f** *kohr•toh m /kohr•tah f /* **largo m /larga f** *lahr•goh m /lahr•gah f*
tight/loose	**ajustado/suelto** *a•hoos•tah•doh/swell•toh*
Do you have this in size…?	**¿Tiene esto en la talla…?** *teeyeh•neh ehs•toh ehn lah tah•yah…*
Do you have this in a bigger/smaller size?	**¿Tiene esto en una talla más grande/ chica?** *teeyeh•neh ehs•toh ehn oo•nah tah•yah mahs grahn•deh/chee•kah*

YOU MAY HEAR…

Se le ve muy bien *Seh leh beh moo-ee byehn*	That looks great on you.
¿Cómo le queda? *Koh•mo leh ke•dah?*	How does it fit?
No lo tenemos en su talla *No loh te•neh•mos ehn soo tah•yah*	We don't have your size.

YOU MAY SEE…

ROPA DE CABALLERO	men's clothing
ROPA DE DAMA	women's clothing
ROPA DE NIÑOS	children's clothing

Colors

I'd like something...	**Busco algo...** *boos·koh ahl·goh...*
beige	**beige** *beh·eesh*
black	**negro** *neh·groh*
blue	**azul** *ah·sool*
brown	**café** *kah·feh*
green	**verde** *behr·deh*
gray	**gris** *grees*
orange	**naranja** *nah·rahn·khah*
pink	**rosa** *rroh·sah*
purple	**morado** *moh·rah·doh*
red	**rojo** *rroh·khoh*
white	**blanco** *blahn·koh*
yellow	**amarillo** *ah·mah·ree·yoh*

Clothes & Accessories

a backpack	**la mochila** *lah moh·chee·lah*
a belt	**el cinturón** *ehl seen·too·rohn*
a bikini	**el bikini** *ehl bee·kee·nee*
a blouse	**la blusa** *lah bloo·sah*
a bra	**el sostén** *ehl sohs·tehn*
briefs [underpants]/ panties	**los calzones** *lohs kahl·sohn·nehs*
a coat	**el abrigo** *ehl ah·bree·goh*
a dress	**el vestido** *ehl behs·tee·doh*
a hat	**el sombrero** *ehl sohm·breh·roh*
a jacket	**la chamarra** *lah chah·mah·rrah*
jeans	**los jeans** *lohs jeens*
pajamas	**la piyama** *lah pee·yhah·mah*
pants [trousers]	**los pantalones** *lohs pahn·tah·loh·nehs*
pantyhose [tights]	**las medias** *lahs meh·deeyahs*

a purse [handbag]	**la bolsa** *lah bohl·sah*
a raincoat	**el impermeable** *ehl eem·pehr·meh·ah·bleh*
a scarf	**la bufanda** *lah boo·fahn·dah*
a shirt	**la camisa** *lah kah·mee·sah*
shorts	**los pantaloncillos** *lohs pahn·tah·lohn·see·yohs*
a skirt	**la falda** *lah fahl·dah*
socks	**los calcetines** *lohs kahl·seh·tee·nehs*
a suit	**el traje** *ehl trah·kheh*
sunglasses	**los lentes oscuros** *lohs lehn·tehs ohs·koo·rohs*
a sweater	**el suéter** *ehl sweh·tehr*
a sweatshirt	**la sudadera** *lah soo·dah·deh·rah*
a swimsuit	**el traje de baño** *ehl trah·kheh deh bah·nyoh*
a T-shirt	**la playera** *lah plah·yeh·rah*
a tie	**la corbata** *lah kohr·bah·tah*
underwear	**la ropa interior**
	lah rroh·pah een·teh·reeyohr

Fabric

I'd like…	**Quiero…** *keeyeh·roh…*
cotton	**algodón** *ahl·goh·dohn*
denim	**mezclilla** *mehs·klee·yah*
lace	**encaje** *ehn·kah·kheh*

leather	**cuero** *kweh·roh*
linen	**lino** *lee·noh*
silk	**seda** *seh·dah*
wool	**lana** *lah·nah*
Is it machine washable?	**¿Se puede lavar en lavadora?** *seh pweh·deh lah·bahr ehn lah·bah·doh·rah*

Shoes

I'd like...	**Quiero...** *keeyeh·roh...*
high-heels/flats	**zapatos de tacón/planos** *sah·pah·tohs deh tah·kohn/plah·nohs*
boots	**botas** *boh·tahs*
loafers	**mocasines** *moh·kah·see·nehs*
sandals	**sandalias** *sahn·dah·leeyahs*
shoes	**zapatos** *sah·pah·tohs*
slippers	**pantuflas** *pahn·too·flahs*
sneakers	**tenis** *teh·nees*
Size...	**Tiene en talla...** *tee·eh·neh ehn tah·yah...*

For Numbers, see page 167.

Sizes

small (S)	**pequeña (S)** *peh·keh·nyah (eh·seh)*
medium (M)	**mediana (M)** *meh·deeyah·nah (eh·meh)*
large (L)	**grande (L)** *grahn·deh (eh·leh)*
extra large (XL)	**extra grande** *ehks·trah grahn·deh*
petite	**petite** *peh·teet*
plus size	**tallas extra** *tah·yahs ehks·trah*

Newsagent & Tobacconist

Do you sell English-language newspapers?	**¿Venden periódicos en inglés?** *behn·dehn peh·reeyoh·dee·kohs ehn een·glehs*
I'd like...	**Quiero...** *keeyeh·roh...*
candy [sweets]	**dulces** *dool·sehs*
chewing gum	**chicle** *chee·kleh*
a chocolate bar	**un chocolate** *oon choh·koh·lah·teh*
a cigar	**un puro** *oon poo·roh*
a pack/carton of cigarettes	**una cajetilla/caja de cigarros** *oo·nah kah·kheh·tee·yah/kah·khah deh see·gah·rrohs*
a lighter	**un encendedor** *oon ehn·sehn·deh·dohr*
a magazine	**una revista** *oo·nah rreh·bees·tah*
matches	**los cerillos** *lohs seh·ree·yohs*
a newspaper	**un periódico** *oon peh·reeyoh·dee·koh*
a pen	**una pluma** *oo·nah ploo·mah*
a postcard	**una postal** *oo·nah pohs·tahl*
a road/town map of...	**un mapa de carreteras/poblaciones de...** *oon mah·pah deh kah·rreh·teh·rahs/ poh·blah·seeoh·nehs deh...*
stamps	**estampillas** *ehs·tahm·pee·yahs*

Mexican culture today is the result of the rise and fall of its numerous Amerindian civilizations combined with 300 years of Spanish rule. This **eclecticism** is clearly visible in Mexican art. **Folk art**, such as pottery, carvings or metal work, is extremely popular and pieces are available for viewing in museums and for purchase throughout the country. You can also see Mexican tradition reflected in the works of the many modern Mexican painters such as the famous muralists, **José Clemente Orozco, Diego Rivera** and **David Alfaro Siqueiros,** or **Rufino Tamayo** and **Frida Kahlo.** In Mexico City, exhibitions by these artists are on display in the **Bellas Artes Museum, the Modern Art Museum** or the **Carrillo Gil Museum;** both **Rivera** and **Tamayo** have their own museums as well.

Photography

I'd like…camera.	**Quiero una cámara…**
	keeyeh·roh oo·nah kah·mah·rah…
an automatic	**automática**
	awoo·toh·mah·tee·kah
a digital	**digita**l *dee·khee·tahl*
a disposable	**desechable** d*eh·seh·chah·bleh*
I'd like…	**Quiero…** *keeyeh·roh…*
a battery	**una batería**
	oo·nah bah·teh·ree·ah
digital prints	**fotos digitales**
	foh·tohs dee·khee·tah·lehs
a memory card	**una tarjeta de memoria**
	oo·nah tahr·kheh·tah deh meh·moh·reeyah
Can I print digital photos here?	**¿Puedo imprimir aquí fotos digitales?** *pweh·doh*
	eem·pree·meer ah·kee foh·tohs dee·khee·tah·lehs

Souvenirs

a bottle of wine	**una botella de vino** *oonah boh•teh•yah deh bee•noh*
a box of chocolates	**una caja de chocolates** *oonah kah•khah deh choh•koh•lah•tehs*
some crystal	**algún cristal** *ahl•goon krees•tahl*
a doll	**una muñeca mexicana** *oonah moo•nyeh•kah meh•khee•cah•nah*
some jewelry	**alguna joya** *al•goo•nah hoh•jah*
a key ring	**un llavero** *oon yah•beh•roh*
a postcard	**una postal** *oonah pohs•tahl*
some pottery	**algo de cerámica** *ahl•goh deh seh•rah•mee•kah*
a T-shirt	**una playera** *oonah plah•yeh•rah*
a toy	**un juguete** *oon khoo•geh•teh*
Can I see this/that?	**¿Puedo ver esto/eso?** *pweh•doh behr ehs•toh/eh•soh*
I'd like…	**Quiero…** *keeyeh•roh…*
a battery	**una pila** *oo•nah pee•lah*
a bracelet	**una pulsera** *oo•nah pool•seh•rah*
a brooch	**un prendedor** *oon prehn•deh•dohr*
a clock	**un reloj** *oon rre•lohkh*
earrings	**unos aretes** *oo•nohs ah•reh•tehs*

a necklace	**un collar** *oon koh•yahr*
a ring	**un anillo** *oon ah•nee•yoh*
a watch	**un reloj de pulsera** *oon rreh•lohkh deh pool•seh•rah*
I'd like…	**Quiero…** *keeyeh•roh…*
copper	**cobre** *koh•breh*
crystal	**cristal** *krees•tahl*
diamonds	**diamantes** *deeyah•mahn•tehs*
white/yellow gold	**oro blanco/amarillo** *oh•roh blahn•koh/ahmah•ree•yoh*
pearls	**perlas** *pehr•lahs*
pewter	**pewter** *peh•oo•tehr*
platinum	**platino** *plah•tee•noh*
sterling silver	**plata de ley** *plah•tah deh lehee*
Is this real?	**¿Es auténtico?** *ehs awoo•tehn•tee•koh*
Can you engrave it?	**¿Puede grabármelo?** *pweh•deh grah•bahr•meh•loh*

For Colors, see page 124.

Sport & Leisure

ESSENTIAL

When's the game?	**¿Cuándo empieza el partido?** *kwahn·doh ehm·peeyeh·sah ehl pahr·tee·doh*
Where's…?	**¿Dónde está…?** *dohn·deh ehs·tah…*
the beach	**la playa** *lah plah·yah*
the park	**el parque** *ehl pahr·keh*
the pool	**la alberca** *lah ahl·behr·kah*
Is it safe to swim here?	**¿Es seguro nadar aquí?** *ehs seh·goo·roh nah·dahr ah·kee*
Can I hire clubs?	**¿Puedo rentar palos de golf?** *pweh·doh rrehn·tahr pah·lohs deh golf*
How much per hour/day?	**¿Cuánto cuesta por hora?** *kwahn·toh kwehs·tah pohr oh·rah*
How far is it to…?	**¿A qué distancia está…?** *ah keh dees·tahn·seeyah ehs·tah…*
Show me on the map, please.	**¿Puede indicármelo en el mapa, por favor?** *pweh·deh een·dee·kahr·meh·loh ehn ehl mah·pah pohr fah·bohr*

Fútbol (soccer) is the most popular sport in Mexico; most of the major cities in Mexico have their own professional teams with a large fan base. Note that fans are extremely dedicated, so be sure not to insult the team. Other popular sports include **fútbol americano** (American football), **básquetbol** (basketball), **boxeo** (boxing), **los toros** or **la fiesta brava** (bullfighting) and **lucha libre** (freestyle wrestling).

Watching Sport

When's...(game/race/	¿Cuándo empieza...?
tournament)?	*kwahn·doh ehm·peeyeh·sah...*
the baseball	**el partido de béisbol** *ehl pahr·tee·doh deh base·ball*
the basketball	**el partido de básquetbol**
	ehl pahr·tee·doh deh bahs·keht·bohl
the boxing	**la pelea de box** *lah peh·leh·ah deh bohx*
the cricket	**el partido de cricket** *el pahrteedoh deh cricket*
the cycling	**la carrera de bicicletas**
	lah kha·rreh·rah deh bee·see·kleh·tahs
the golf	**el torneo de golf** *ehl tohr·neh·oh deh golf*
the soccer [football]	**el partido de fútbol** *ehl pahr·tee·doh deh foot·bohl*
the tennis	**el partido de tenis** *ehl pahr·tee·doh deh teh·nees*
the volleyball	**el partido de voleibol**
	ehl pahr·tee·doh deh boh·lehee·bohl
Who's playing?	**¿Quiénes juegan?** *keeyeh·nehs khweh·gahn*
Where's the racetrack	**¿Dónde está...?** *dohn·deh ehs·tah...*
/stadium ?	**la pista de carreras/estadio**
	lah pees·tah de kah·rreh·rahs/ehs·tah·dyoh
Where can I place	**¿Dónde puedo hacer una apuesta?**
a bet?	*dohn·deh pweh·doh ah·sehr oo·nah ah·pwehs·tah*

For Tickets, see page 19.

Playing Sport

Where is/are...?	**¿Dónde está/están...?**
	dohn·deh ehs·tah/ ehs·tahn...
the golf course	**el campo de golf** *ehl kahm·poh deh golf*
the gym	**el gimnasio** *ehl kheem·nah·seeyoh*
the park	**el parque** *ehl pahr·keh*
the tennis courts	**las canchas de tenis** *lahs kahn·chahs deh teh·nees*
How much per...	**¿Cuánto cuesta por...?** *kwahn·toh kwehs·tah pohr...*

day	**día** dee·ah
hour	**hora** oh·rah
game	**partido** pahr·tee·doh
round	**juego** khweh·goh
Can I rent [hire]...?	**¿Puedo rentar...?** pweh·doh rrehn·tahr...
some clubs	**palos de golf** pah·lohs deh golf
some equipment	**equipo** eh·kee·poh
a racket	**una raqueta** oo·nah rrah·keh·tah

At the Beach/Pool

Where's the beach/pool?	**¿Dónde está la playa/alberca?** dohn·deh ehs·tah lah plah·yah/ahl·behr·kah
Is there a...?	**¿Hay...?** aye...
kiddie pool	**un chapoteadero** oon chah·poh·teh·ah·deh·roh
indoor/outdoor pool	**una alberca cubierta/exterior** oo·nah ahl·behr·kah koo·beeyehr·tah/ehx·teh·reeyohr
lifeguard	**un salvavidas** oon sahl·bah·bee·dahs
Is it safe...?	**¿Es seguro...?** ehs seh·goo·roh...
to swim	**nadar** nah·dahr
to dive	**tirarse un clavado** tee·rahr·seh oon klah·bah·doh
for children	**para los niños** pah·rah lohs nee·nyohs

I'd like to hire...	**Quiero rentar...** *keeyeh·roh rrehn·tahr...*
a deck chair	**un camastro** *oon kah·mahs·troh*
diving equipment	**equipo de buceo** *eh·kee·poh deh boo·seh·oh*
a jet ski	**una moto acuática** *oo·nah moh·toh ah·kwah·tee·kah*
a motorboat	**una lancha de motor** *oo·nah lahn·chah deh moh·tohr*
a rowboat	**un bote de remos** *oon boh·teh deh rreh·mohs*
snorkeling equipment	**equipo de esnórquel** *eh·kee·poh deh ehz·nohr·kehl*
a surfboard	**una tabla de surf** *oo·nah tah·blah deh soorf*
a towel	**una toalla** *oo·nah toh·ah·yah*
an umbrella	**una sombrilla** *oo·nah sohm·bree·yah*
water skis	**unos esquís acuáticos** *oo·nohs ehs·kees ah·kwah·tee·kohs*
a windsurfing board	**una tabla de windsurf** *oo·nah tah·blah deh weend·soorf*
For...hours.	**Por...horas.** *pohr...oh·rahs*

For Watching Sport, see page 132.

Mexico has many miles of coastline and beaches, boasting
some of the most beautiful beaches in the **Caribbean (Cancún,
Cozumel, the Mayan Riviera)** and the **Pacific Coast (Huatulco,
Ixtapa, Puerto Vallarta)**. If you decide to go for a swim, check the
safety flags at each beach. Green flags indicate the water is safe, yellow
flags indicate that you should use caution and red flags indicate that
the water is unsafe for swimming.

Out in the Country

A map of..., please.	**Un mapa de..., por favor.**
	oon mah•pah deh...pohr fah•bohr
this region	**esta región** *ehs•tah rreh•kheeyohn*
the walking routes	**las rutas de caminata**
	lahs rroo•tahs deh kah•mee•nah•tah
the bike routes	**las rutas para bicicletas**
	lahs rroo•tahs pah•rah bee•see•kleh•tahs
the trails	**los senderos** *lohs sehn•deh•rohs*
Is it...?	
easy/difficult	**¿Es fácil/difícil?** *ehs fah•seel/dee•fee•seel*
far/steep	**¿Está lejos/empinado?**
	ehs•tah leh•khohs/ehm•pee•nah•doh
How far is it to...?	**¿A qué distancia está...?**
	ah keh dees•tahn•seeyah ehs•tah...
I'm lost.	**Me perdí.** *meh pehr•dee*
Where's...?	**¿Dónde está...?** *dohn•deh ehs•tah...*
the bridge	**el puente** *ehl pwehn•teh*
the cave	**la cueva** *lah kweh•bah*
the desert	**el desierto** *ehl deh•seeyehr•toh*
the farm	**la granja** *lah grahn•khah*

the field	**el campo** *ehl kahm·poh*
the forest	**el bosque** *ehl bohs·keh*
the hill	**el cerro** *ehl seh·rroh*
the lake	**el lago** *ehl lah·goh*
the mountain	**la montaña** *lah mohn·tah·nyah*
the nature preserve	**la reserva natural** *lah rreh·sehr·bah nah·too·rahl*
the viewpoint	**el mirador** *ehl mee·rah·dohr*
the park	**el parque** *ehl pahr·keh*
the path	**el camino** *ehl kah·mee·noh*
the peak	**el pico** *ehl pee·koh*
the picnic area	**el área para día de campo** *ehl ah·reh·ah pah·rah dee·ah deh kahm·poh*
the pond	**el estanque** *ehl ehs·tahn·keh*
the river	**el río** *ehl rree·oh*
the sea	**el mar** *ehl mahr*
the (hot) spring	**el manantial (de aguas termales)** *ehl mah·nahn·teeyahl (deh ah·gwahs tehr·mah·lehs)*
the stream	**el arroyo** *ehl ah·rroh·yoh*
the valley	**el valle** *ehl bah·yeh*
the vineyard	**el viñedo** *ehl bee·nyeh·doh*
the waterfall	**la cascada** *lah kahs·kah·dah*

Mexico has no shortage of great outdoor sports amenities thanks to its privileged location and biodiversity. You can explore it by train, horse or bicycle, on foot or by kayak, camping or climbing mountains.

Going Out

ESSENTIAL

What's there to do at night?	**¿Qué se puede hacer en la noche?** *keh seh pweh·deh ah·sehr ehn lah noh·cheh*
Do you have a program of events?	**¿Tiene un programa de eventos?** *teeyeh·neh oon proh·grah·mah deh eh·behn·tohs*
What's playing tonight?	**¿Qué hay en cartelera esta noche?** *keh aye ehn kahr·teh·leh·rah ehs·tah noh·cheh*
Where's...?	**¿Dónde está...?** *dohn·deh ehs·tah...*
the downtown area	**el centro** *ehl sehn·troh*
the bar	**el bar** *ehl bahr*
the dance club	**la discoteca** *lah dees·koh·teh·kah*

Entertainment

Can you recommend...?	**¿Puede recomendarme...?** *pweh·deh rreh·koh·mehn·dahr·meh...*
a concert	**un concierto** *oon kohn·seeyehr·toh*
a movie	**una película** *oo·nah peh·lee·koo·lah*
an opera	**una ópera** *oo·nah oh·peh·rah*
a play	**una obra de teatro** *oo·nah oh·brah deh teh·ah·trohs*
When does it start /end ?	**¿A qué hora empieza/termina?** *ah keh oh·rah ehm·peeyeh·sah/tehr·mee·nah*
What's the dress code?	**¿Cómo hay que ir vestido *m* /vestida *f* ?** *koh·moh aye keh eer behs·tee·doh /behs·tee·dah*
I like...	**Me gusta...** *meh goos·tah...*
classical music	**la música clásica** *lah moo·see·kah klah·see·kah*
folk music	**la música folclórica** *lah moo·see·kahfohl·kloh·ree·kah*
jazz	**el jazz** *ehl jahzz*

The **mariachi** is a type of musical group, originally from **Cocula, Jalisco.** Usually a **mariachi** band (also known as **los mariachis**) consists of violins, trumpets, guitars, **vihuela** (a high-pitched, five string guitar) and **guitarrón** (an acoustic bass). Professional mariachis are normally singers skilled at playing more than one instrument. Trios or larger groups of mariachis (up to 12 band members) can be found for hire for serenading women; the best known venues are **Plaza de los Mariachis** in **Guadalajara** and **Plaza Garibaldi** in downtown **Mexico City**. They are also hired to liven up various celebrations.

Nightlife

What's there to do at night?	**¿Qué se puede hacer en la noche?**
	keh seh pweh·deh ah·sehr ehn lah noh·cheh
Can you recommend…?	**¿Puede recomendarme…?**
	pweh·deh rreh·koh·mehn·dahr·meh…
a bar	**un bar** *oon bahr*
a cabaret	**un cabaret** *oon kah·bah·reht*
a casino	**un casino** *oon kah·see·noh*

a dance club	**una discoteca** *oo·nah dees·koh·teh·kah*
a gay club	**una discoteca gay** *oo·nah dees·koh·teh·kah gay*
a jazz club	**un club de jazz** *oon kloob deh jazz*
a club with traditional Mexican music	**un bar con música típica mexicana** *oon bahr kohn moo·see·kah tee·pee·kah me meh·khee·kah·nah*
Is there live music?	**¿Hay música en vivo?** *aye moo·see·kah ehn bee·boh*
How do I get there?	**¿Cómo llego allí?** *koh·moh yeh·goh ah·yee*
Is there a cover charge?	**¿Hay que pagar cover?** *aye keh pah·gahr koh·behr*
Let's go dancing.	**Vamos a bailar.** *bah·mohs ah bayee·lahr*
Is this area safe at night?	**¿Es ésta un área segura de noche?** *Ehs ehs·ta oon ah·ria seh·goo·rah deh noh·tcheh*

YOU MAY HEAR...

Por favor apaguen sus celulares.
pohr fah·bohr ah·pah·gehn soos sehl·yoo·lah·rehs

Turn off your cell [mobile] phones, please.

Special Requirements

Business Travel 14‌
Traveling with Children 143
Disabled Travelers 146

Business Travel

ESSENTIAL

I'm here on business.	**Estoy aquí en viaje de negocios.**
	ehs•toy ah•kee ehn beeyah•kheh deh neh•goh•seeyohs
Here's my card.	**Aquí tiene mi tarjeta.**
	ah•kee teeyeh•neh mee tahr•kheh•tah
Can I have your card?	**¿Puede darme su tarjeta?**
	pweh•deh dahr•meh soo tahr•kheh•tah
I have a meeting with...	**Tengo una reunión con...**
	tehn•goh oo•nah rrewoo•neeyohn kohn...
Where's...?	**¿Dónde está...?** *dohn•deh ehs•tah...*
the business center	**el centro de negocios**
	ehl sehn•troh deh neh•goh•seeyohs
the convention hall	**el salón de congresos** *ehl sah•lohn deh kohn•greh•sohs*
the meeting room	**la sala de reuniones** *lah sah•lah deh*
	rrewoo•neeyohn•ehs

It is common to greet colleagues with **buenos días** (good morning) and a shake of hands. When leaving, simply say **adiós**, **gracias** or **hasta luego** (goodbye, thank you or see you later).

On Business

I'm here for...	**Estoy aquí para asistir...**
	ehs•toy ah•kee pah•rah ah•sees•teer...
a seminar	**a un seminario** *ah oon seh•mee•nah•reeyoh*
a conference	**a una conferencia** *ah oo•nah kohn•feh•rehn•seeyah*
a meeting	**a una reunión** *ah oo•nah rrewoo•neeyohn*

My name is…	**Me llamo…** *meh yah·moh…*
May I introduce	**Le presento a mi compañero m / compañera f de**
my colleague…	**trabajo…** *leh preh·sehn·toh ah mee*
	kohm·pah·nyeh·roh m /kohm·pah·nyeh·rah f deh
	trah·bah·khoh

I have a meeting/an	**Tengo una reunión/cita con…**
appointment with…	*tehn·goh oo·nah rrewoo·neeyohn/see·tah kohn…*
I'm sorry I'm late.	**Disculpe que haya llegado tarde.**
	dees·kool·peh keh ah·yah yeh·gah·doh tahr·deh

| I need an interpreter. | **Necesito un intérprete.** |
| | *neh·seh·see·toh oon een·tehr·preh·teh* |

You can contact me	**Puede encontrarme en el Hotel…**
at the…Hotel.	*pweh·deh ehn·kohn·trahr·meh ehn ehl oh·tehl…*
I'm here until…	**Estaré aquí hasta…** *ehs·tah·reh ah·kee ahs·tah…*
I need to…	**Necesito…** *neh·seh·see·toh…*
make a call	**hacer una llamada** *ah·sehr oo·nah yah·mah·dah*

YOU MAY HEAR…

¿Tiene cita? *teeyeh·neh see·tah*	Do you have an appointment?
¿Con quién? *kohn keeyehn*	With whom?
Está en una reunión *ehs·tah ehn oo·nah rrewoo·neeyohn*	He/She is in a meeting.
Un momento, por favor. *oon moh·mehn·toh pohr fah·bohr*	One moment, please.
Siéntese. *seeyehn·teh·seh*	Have a seat.
¿Quiere algo de tomar? *keeyeh·reh ahl·goh deh toh·mahr*	Would you like something to drink?
Gracias por su visita. *grah·seeyahs pohr soo bee·see·tah*	Thank you for coming.

make a photocopy	**sacar una fotocopia** *sah•kahr oo•nah foh•toh•koh•peeyah*
send an e-mail	**enviar un correo electrónico**
	ehn•bee•ahr oon koh•rreh•oh ee•lehk•troh•nee•koh
send a fax	**enviar un fax** *ehn•bee•ahr oon fahx*
send a package	**enviar un paquete (para entrega al día**
(for next-day	**siguiente)** *ehn•bee•ahr oon pah•keh•teh (pah•rah*
delivery)	*ehn•treh•gah ahl dee•ah see•geeyehn•teh)*
It was a pleasure to	**Mucho gusto.**
meet you.	*moo•choh goos•toh*

For Communications, see page 48.

Traveling with Children

ESSENTIAL

Is there a discount for kids?	**¿Hacen descuento para niños?** *ah•sen dehs•kwehn•toh pah•rah nee•nyohs*
Can you recommend a babysitter?	**¿Puede recomendarme una niñera?** *pweh•deh rreh•koh•mehn•dahr•meh oo•nah neeh•nyeh•rah*
Do you have a child's seat/highchair?	**¿Tienen una silla para niños/periquera?** *teeyeh•nehn oo•nah see•yah pah•rah nee•nyohs/ peh•ree•keh•rah*
Where can I change the baby?	**¿Dónde puedo cambiar al bebé?** *dohn•deh pweh•doh kahm•beeyahr ahl beh•beh*

Out & About

Can you recommend something for kids?	**¿Puede recomendarme algo para los niños?** *pweh•deh rreh•koh•mehn•dahr•meh ahl•goh pah•rah lohs nee•nyohs*

Where's...?	**¿Dónde está...?** *dohn-deh ehs-tah...*
the amusement park	**el parque de diversiones** *ehl pahr-keh deh dee-behr-seeyoh-nehs*
the arcade	**la sala de videojuegos** *lah sah-lah deh bee-deeoh-khwe-gohs*
the kiddie [paddling] pool	**el chapoteadero** *ehl chah-poh-teh-ah-deh-roh*
the park	**el parque** *ehl pahr-keh*
the playground	**el parque infantil** *ehl pahr-keh een-fahn-teel*
the zoo	**el zoológico** *ehl soh-oh-loh-khee-koh*
Are kids allowed?	**¿Se permite la entrada a niños?** *seh pehr-mee-teh lah ehn-trah-dah ah nee-nyohs*
Is it safe for kids?	**¿Es seguro para niños?** *ehs seh-goo-roh pah-rah nee-nyohs*
Is it suitable for... year olds?	**¿Es adecuado para niños de...años?** *ehs ah-deh-koo-ah-doh pah-rah nee-nyohs deh... ah-nyohs*

For Numbers, see page 167.

YOU MAY HEAR...

¡Qué bonito *m* **/bonita** *f***!**
! keh boh-nee-toh **m** */ boh-nee-tah* **f**

¿Cómo se llama? *koh-moh seh yah-mah*

¿Qué edad tiene? *keh eh-dahd teeyeh-neh*

How cute!

What's his/her name?

How old is he/she?

Baby Essentials

Do you have...?	**¿Tiene...?** *teeyeh-neh...*
a baby bottle	**un biberón** *oon bee-beh-rohn*
baby food	**comida para bebé** *co-mee-dah pahrah beh-beh*

baby wipes	**toallitas para bebé** *toh·ah·yee·tahs pah·rah beh·beh*
a car seat	**un asiento para niños** *oon ah·seeyehn·toh pah·rah nee·nyohs*
a children's menu /portion	**un menú/una ración para niños** *oon meh·noo/oo·nah rrah·seeyohn pah·rah nee·nyohs*
a child's seat/ highchair	**una silla para niños/periquera** *oo·nah see·yah pah·rah nee·nyohs/peh·ree·khe·rah*
a crib/cot	**una cuna/un catre** *oo·nah koo·nah/oon kah·treh*
diapers [nappies]	**pañales** *pah·nyah·lehs*
formula	**fórmula** *fohr·moo·lah*
a pacifier [dummy]	**un chupón** *oon choo·pohn*
a playpen	**un corral** *oon koh·rrahl*
a stroller [pushchair]	**una carriola** *oo·nah kah·rreeyoh·lah*
Can I breastfeed the baby here?	**¿Puedo darle pecho al bebé aquí?** *pweh·doh dahr·leh peh·choh ahl beh·beh ah·kee*
Where can I breastfeed /change the baby?	**¿Dónde puedo cambiar al bebé?** *dohn·deh pweh·doh kahm·beeyahr ahl beh·beh*

For Dining with Children, see page 63.

Babysitting

Can you recommend a babysitter?	**¿Puede recomendarme una niñera?** *pweh·deh rreh·koh·mehn·dahr·meh oo·nah neeh·nyeh·rah*

How much do you/ they charge?	**¿Cuánto cuesta?**
	kwahn·toh kwehs·tah
I'll be back at…	**Vuelvo a la/las…** *bwehl·boh ah lah/lahs…*
If you need to contact me, call…	**Puede encontrarme en el…**
	pweh·deh ehn·kohn·trahr·meh ehn ehl…

For Time, see page 169.

Health & Emergency

Can you recommend a pediatrician?	**¿Puede recomendarme un pediatra?**
	pweh·deh rreh·koh·mehn·dahr·meh oon peh·deeyah·trah
My child is allergic to…	**Mi hijo/hija es alérgico** *m* **/alérgica** *f* **a…**
	mee ee·khoh/ee·khah ehs ah·lehr·khee·koh m /
	ah·lehr·khee·kah f ah…
My child is missing.	**Mi hijo/hija ha desaparecido.**
	mee ee·khoh/ee·khah ah deh·sah·pah·reh·see·doh
Have you seen a boy/girl?	**¿Ha visto a un niño/una niña?**
	ah bees·toh ah oon nee·nyoh/oo·nah nee·nyah

For Health, see page 152.

Disabled Travelers

ESSENTIAL

Is there…?	**¿Hay…?**
	aye…
access for the disabled	**acceso para los discapacitados**
	ahk·seh·soh pah·rah lohs dees·kah·pah·see·tah·dohs
a wheelchair ramp	**una rampa para sillas de ruedas**
	oo·nah rrahm·pah pah·rah see·yahs deh rrweh·dahs

a disabled- accessible toilet	**un baño con acceso para discapacitados** *oon bah·nyoh kohn ahk·seh·soh pah·rah* *dees·kah·pah·see·tah·dohs*
I need...	**Necesito...** *neh·seh·see·toh...*
assistance	**ayuda** *ah·yoo·dah*
an elevator [a lift]	**un elevador** *oon eh·leh·bah·dohr*
a ground-floor room	**una habitación en la planta baja** *oo·nah ah·bee·tah·seeyohn ehn lah plahn·tah*

Asking for Assistance

I'm... disabled	**Soy discapacitado** *m* **/discapacitada** *f*.
visually impaired/ hearing impaired	**Tengo discapacidad visual/auditiva** *tehn·goh dees·kah·pah·see·dahd bee·swahl/* *awoo·dee·tee·bah*
deaf	**Soy sordo** *f*. *soy sohr·doh m /sohr·dah f*
unable to walk far/ use the stairs	**No puedo caminar muy lejos/subir las escaleras.** *noh pweh·doh kah·mee·nahr mooyee leh·khohs/* *soo·beer lahs ehs·kah·leh·rahs*
Please speak louder.	**Por favor hable más fuerte.** *Pohr fah·bohr ah·bleh mahs foo·ehr·teh*
Can I bring my wheelchair?	**¿Puedo traer la silla de ruedas?** *pweh·doh trah·ehr lah see·yah deh rrweh·dahs*
Are guide dogs permitted?	**¿Permiten a perros guía?** *pehr·mee·tehn ah peh·rrohs gee·ah*
Can you help me?	**¿Puede ayudarme?** *pweh·deh ah·yoo·dahr·meh*
Please open/hold the door.	**Por favor, abra/detenga la puerta.** *pohr fah·bohr ah·brah/deh·tehn·gah lah pwehr·tah*

For Police, see page 150.

In an Emergency

Emergencies	149
Police	150
Health	152
The Basics	162

Emergencies

ESSENTIAL

Help!	**¡Auxilio!**
	aw•xee•leeyoh
Go away!	**¡Váyase!**
	bah•yah•seh
Stop, thief!	**¡Alto, ladrón!**
	ahl•toh lah•drohn
Get a doctor!	**¡Llame a un doctor!**
	yah•meh ah oon dohk•tohr
Fire!	**¡Fuego!**
	fweh•goh
I'm lost.	**Me perdí.**
	meh pehr•dee
Can you help me?	**¿Puede ayudarme?**
	pweh•deh ah•yoo•dahr•meh

The emergency number in Mexico varies depending on the state you are in so it is best to check this on arrival. For the police and emergency services, **dial 060 (Mexico City and many other states).** In some parts of Mexico, you will need to **dial 066 (Yucatán).**

Police

ESSENTIAL

Call the police!	**¡Llame a la policía!** yah•meh ah lah poh•lee•see•ah
Where's the police station?	**¿Dónde está la estación de policia?** dohn•deh ehs•tah lah ehs•tah•seeyohn deh poh•lee•see•ah
There was an accident/attack.	**Hubo un accidente/asalto** ooh•boh oon ahk•see•dehn•teh/ah•sahl•toh
My child is missing.	**Mi hijo/hija desapareció.** mee ee•khoh/ee•khah deh•sah•pah•reh•seeyoh
I need...	**Necesito...** neh•seh•see•toh...
an interpreter	**un intérprete** oon een•tehr•preh•teh
to make a phone call.	**hacer una llamada** ah•sehr oo•nah yah•mah•dah
I'm innocent.	**Soy inocente.** soy ee•noh•sehn•teh

YOU MAY HEAR...

Llene este formulario yeh•neh ehs•teh fohr•mooh•lah•reeoh	Fill out this form.
Su identificación, por favor. soo ee•dehn•tee•fee•kah•seeyohn pohr fah•bohr	Your ID, please.
¿Cuándo/Dónde ocurrió? ? kwahn•doh/dohn•deh oh•koo•rreeyoh	When/Where did it happen?
¿Puede describirlo m /describirla f ? ? pweh•deh dehs•kree•beer•loh m / dehs•kree•beer•lah f	What does he/she look like?

Crime & Lost Property

I'd like to report...	**Quiero denunciar...**
	keeyeh·rohdeh·noon·seeyahr...
a mugging	**un asalto** *oo·n ah·sahl· toh*
a rape	**una violación** *oo·nah beeyoh·lah·seeyohn*
a theft	**un robo** *oon rroh·boh*
I was mugged/	**Me asaltaron/atracaron.**
I was robbed.	*meh ah·sahl·tah·rohn/ah·trah·kah·rohn*
I lost...	**Perdí mi...** *pehr·dee mee...*
...was stolen.	**Me robaron...** *meh rroh·bah·rohn...*
My backpack	**la mochila** *lah moh·chee·lah*
My bicycle	**la bicicleta** *lah bee·see·kleh·tah*
My camera	**la cámara** *lah kah·mah·rah*
My (hire) car	**el auto rentado**
	ehl awoo·toh (rrehn·tah·doh)
My computer	**la computadora**
	lah kohm·poo·tah·doh·rah
My credit card	**la tarjeta de crédito**
	lah tahr·kheh·tah deh kreh·dee·toh
My jewelry	**las joyas** *lahs khoh·yahs*
My money	**el dinero** *ehl dee·neh·roh*
My passport	**el pasaporte** *ehl pah·sah·pohr·teh*
My purse [handbag]	**el bolso** *ehl bohl·soh*
My traveller's	**los cheques de viajero**
cheques	*lohs cheh·kehs deh beeyah·kheh·roh*
My wallet	**la cartera** *lah kahr·teh·rah*
I need a police	**Necesito un acta ministerial.**
report.	*neh·seh·see·toh oon ahk·tah mee·nees·teh·reeyahl*
Where is the British/	**¿Dónde está la embajada británica/americana/**
American/Irish	**irlandesa?** *dohn·deh ehs·tah lah ehm·ba·hah·dah*
embassy?	*bree·tah·nee·kah/ahme·ree·cah·nah/eer·lan·day·sah*

Health

ESSENTIAL

I'm sick	**Me siento mal.** *meh seeyehn·toh mahl*
I need an English-speaking doctor	**Necesito un doctor que hable inglés.** *neh·seh·see·toh oon dohk·tohr keh ah·bleh een·glehs*
It hurts here.	**Me duele aquí.** *meh dweh·leh ah·kee*

Finding a Doctor

Can you recommend a doctor/dentist?	**¿Puede recomendarme un doctor/dentista?** *pweh·dehrreh·koh·mehn·dahr·mehoon dohk·tohr/ dehn·tees·tah*
Can the doctor come here?	**¿Podría el doctor venir aquí?** *poh·dree·ah ehl dohk·tohr beh·neer ah·kee*
I need an English-speaking doctor.	**Necesito un doctor que hable inglés** *neh·seh·see·toh oon dohk·tohr kehah·bleh een·glehs*
What are the office hours?	**¿Cuáles son las horas de consulta?** *kwah·lehs sohn lahs oh·rahs deh kohn·sool·tah*
I'd like an appointment for...	**Quiero una cita...** *keeyeh·roh oo·nah see·tah...*
today	**para hoy** *pah·rah oy*
tomorrow	**para mañana** *pah·rah mah·nyah·nah*
as soon as possible	**lo antes posible** *loh ahn·tehs poh·see·bleh*
It's urgent.	**Es urgente.** *ehs oor·khehn·teh*

Symptoms

I'm bleeding.	**Estoy... sangrando** *ehs·toy... sahn·grahn·doh*
I'm constipated.	**Estoy... estreñido** m **/estreñida** f *ehs·toy... ehs·treh·nyee·doh /ehs·treh·nyee·dah*

I'm dizzy.	**Estoy… mareado** *m* **/mareada** *f*
	ehs•toy…mah•reh•ah•doh /mah•reh•ah•dah
I'm nauseous/	**Tengo náuseas/vómitos.**
I'm vomiting.	*tehn•goh naw•seh•ahs/boh•mee•tohs*
It hurts here.	**Me duele aquí.** *meh dweh•leh ah•kee*
I have…	**Tengo…** *tehn•goh…*
an allergic	**una reacción alérgica**
reaction	*oo•nah rreh•ahk•seeyohn ah•lehr•khee•kah*
chest pain	**dolor de pecho** *doh•lohr deh peh•choh*
cramps	**calámbres** *cah•lahm•brehs*
diarrhea	**diarrea** *dee•ah•rreh•ah*
an earache	**dolor de oído** *doh•lohr deh oh•ee•doh*
a fever	**fiebre** *feeyeh•breh*
pain	**dolor** *doh•lohr*
a rash	**un salpullido** *oon sahl•poo•yee•doh*
a sprain	**un esguince** *oon ehz•geen•seh*
some swelling	**una hinchazón** *oo•nah een•chah•sohn*
a sore throat	**dolor de garganta** *doh•lohr deh gahr-gahn-tah*
a stomachache	**dolor de estómago** *doh•lohr deh ehs•toh•mah•goh*
I've been sick for…	**Hace…días que me siento mal.**
days.	*ah•seh…dee•ahs keh meh seeh•ehn•toh mahl*

For Numbers, see page 167.

Conditions

I'm...	**Soy...** *soy...*
anemic	**anémico** *m* /**anémica** *f*
	ah·neh·mee·koh /*ah·neh·mee·kah*
asthmatic	**asmático** *m* /**asmática** *f*
	ahz·mah·tee·koh /*ahz·mah·tee·kah*
diabetic	**diabético** *m* /**diabética** *f*
	deeyah·beh·tee·koh /*deeyah·beh·tee·kah*
epileptic	**epiléptico** *m* /**epiléptica** *f*
	ehpee·lehp·tee·koh /*ehpee·lehp·tee·kah*
I'm allergic to	**Soy alérgico** *m* /**alérgica** *f* **a los antibióticos/**
antibiotics/penicillin.	**la penicilina.** *soy ah·lehr·khee·koh/*
	ah·lehr·khee·kah ah lohs ahn·tee·beeyoh·tee·kohs/
	lah peh·nee·see·lee·nah
I have...	**Tengo...** *tehn·goh...*
arthritis	**artritis** *ahr·tree·tees*
a heart condition	**Padezco del corazón.** *pah·dehs·koh dehl koh·rah·son*
high/low blood	**la presión alta** *lah preh·seeyohn ahl·tah/*
pressure	*la presión baja lah preh·seeyohn bah·khah*
I'm on...	**Estoy tomando...** *ehs·toy toh·mahn·doh...*

YOU MAY HEAR...

¿Qué le pasa? *keh leh pah·sah* — What's wrong?

¿Dónde le duele? *dohn·deh leh dweh·leh* — Where does it hurt?

¿Le duele aquí? *leh dweh·leh ah·kee* — Does it hurt here?

¿Está tomando algún medicamento? — Are you on medication?
ehs·tah toh·mahn·doh ahl·goon meh·dee·kah·mehn·toh

¿Es alérgico *m* /alérgica *f* a algo? *ehs ah·lehr* — Are you allergic to anything?
·khee·koh/ah·lehr·khee·kah ah ahl·goh

Abra la boca. *ah·brah lah boh·kah* — Open your mouth.

Respire hondo. *rrehs·pee·reh ohn·doh* — Breathe deeply.

Tosa, por favor *to·sah por fah·bohr* — Cough, please.

Tiene que ir al hospital. — Go to the hospital.
teeyeh·neh keh eer ahl ohs·pee·tahl

Treatment

Do I need a prescription/medicine?	**¿Necesito receta/medicina?** *Neh·seh·see·toh reh·seht·ah/meh·dee·see·nah*
Can you prescribe a generic drug?	**¿Me puede recetar una medicina genérica?** *Meh pweh·deh rreh·seh·tahr oonah meh·dee·see·nah heh·neh·ree·kah*
Where can I get it?	**¿Donde la puedo comprar?** *Don·deh lah pueh·doh kom·prahr*

For What to Take, see page 158.

Hospital

Notify my family, please.	**Por favor, avise a mi familia.** *pohr fah·bohr ah·bee·seh ah mee fah·mee·leeyah*

I'm in pain.	**Tengo dolor.** *tehn·goh doh·lohr*
I need a doctor/ nurse.	**Necesito un doctor/una enfermera.** *neh·seh·see·toh oon dohk·tohr/oo·nah ehn·fehr·meh·rah*
When are visiting hours?	**¿Cuál es el horario de visitas?** *kwal ehs ehl oh·rah·ree·oh deh bee·see·tahs*
I'm visiting…	**Vengo a hacer una visita a…** *behn·goh ah ah·sehr oo·nah bee·see·tah ah…*

Dentist

I have… a broken tooth/ a lost filling	**Se me rompió un diente/cayó un empaste.** *seh meh rrohm·peeyoh oon deeyehn·teh/kah·yoh oon ehm·pahs·teh*
a toothache	**Tengo dolor de muelas.** *tehn·goh doh·lohr deh mweh·lahs*
Can you fix this denture?	**¿Puede arreglarme la dentadura postiza?** *pweh·deh ah·rreh·glahr·meh lah dehn·tah·doo·rah pohs·tee·sah*

Gynecologist

I have cramps/a infection.	**Tengo dolores menstruales/una infección vaginal.** *tehn·goh doh·loh·rehs mehns·trwah·lehs/ oo·nah een·fehk·seeyohn bah·khee·nahl*
I missed my period.	**No me ha bajado la regla.** *noh meh ahbah·khah·doh lah rreh·glah*
I'm on the Pill.	**Tomo anticonceptivos.** *toh·moh ahn·tee·kohn·sehp·tee·bohs*
I'm (…months) pregnant.	**Tengo (…meses) de embarazo.** *Tehn·goh (…meh·sehs) deh ehm·bah·rah·soh*
I'm not pregnant.	**No estoy embarazada.** *Noh ehs·toy ehm·bah·rah·sah·dah*
My last period was…	**La última vez que me bajó la regla fue…** *lah ool·tee·mah behs keh meh bah·khoh lah rreh·glah fweh…*

Optician

I lost...	**Perdí...** *pehr•dee...*
a contact lens	**un lente de contacto**
	oon lehn•teh deh kohn•tahk•toh
my glasses	**los anteojos**
	lohs ahn•teh•oh•khos
a lens	**una lente**
	oo•nah lehn•teh

Payment & Insurance

How much?	**¿Cuánto es?** *kwahn•toh ehs*
Can I pay by credit card?	**¿Puedo pagar con tarjeta de crédito?**
	pweh•doh pah•gahr kohn tahr•kheh•tah deh kreh•dee•toh
I have insurance.	**Tengo seguro médico.**
	tehn•goh seh•goo•roh meh•dee•koh
I need a receipt for my insurance.	**Necesito una factura para el seguro médico.** *neh•seh•see•toh oo•nah fahk•too•rah pah•rah ehl seh•goo•roh meh•dee•koh*

Pharmacy

ESSENTIAL

Where's the pharmacy?	**¿Dónde está la farmacia?** *dohn·deh ehs·tah lah fahr·mah·seeyah*
What time does it open/close?	**¿A qué hora abre/cierra?** *ah keh oh·rah ah·breh/seeyeh·rrah*
What would you recommend for…?	**¿Qué me recomienda para…?** *keh meh rreh·koh·meeyehn·dah pah·rah…*
How much do I take?	**¿Qué dosis tomo?** *keh doh·sees toh·moh*
I'm allergic to…	**Soy alérgico m /alérgica f a** *… soy ah·lehr·khee·koh m /ah·lehr·khee·kah f ah…*

There is a wide variety of pharmacies in Mexico, including generic drugstores which sell unbranded medication only. Most drugstores offer a variety of toiletries and other goods, in addition to dispensing medicines. **Business hours are usually from 9:00 a.m. until 7:00 p.m.** In smaller towns, pharmacies may close during lunch time. There are **24-hour pharmacies** available in larger cities.

What to Take

How much do I take?	**¿Qué dosis tomo?** *keh doh·sees toh·moh*
How often?	**¿Con qué frecuencia?** *kohn kehfreh·kwehn·seeyah*
Is it safe for children?	**¿Es adecuado para niños?** *ehs ah·deh·kwah·doh pah·rah nee·nyohs*
I'm taking…	**Estoy tomando…** *ehs·toy toh·mahn·doh…*
Are there side effects?	**¿Tiene algún efecto secundario?** *teeyeh·neh ahl·goon eh·fehk·toh seh·koon·dah·reeyoh*

I need something for…	**Necesito algo para…** *neh•seh•see•toh ahl•goh pah•rah…*
a cold	**el catarro** *ehl kah•tah•rroh*
a cough	**la tos** *lah tohs*
diarrhea	**la diarrea** *lah deeyah•rreh•ah*
a headache	**el dolor de cabeza** *ehl doh•lohr deh cah•beh•sah*
insect bites	**las picaduras de insecto** *lahs pee•kah•doo•rahs deh een•sehk•toh*
motion sickness	**el mareo** *ehl mah•reh•oh*

YOU MAY SEE…

UNA VEZ / TRES VECES AL DÍA	once/three times a day
PASTILLA	tablets
GOTA	drop
CUCHARADITA	teaspoon
DESPUÉS DE / ANTES DE / CON LAS COMIDAS	after/before/with meals
CON EL ESTÓMAGO VACÍO	on an empty stomach
TRAGUE LA PASTILLA ENTERA	swallow whole
PUEDE CAUSAR SUEÑO	may cause drowsiness
NO INGERIR	do not ingest

a sore throat	**las anginas** *lahs ahn·khee·nahs*
sunburn	**las quemaduras del sol**
	lahs keh·mah·doo·rahs deh sohl
a toothache	**el dolor de muelas** *ehl doh·lohr deh mweh·lahs*
an upset stomach	**el malestar estomacal**
	ehl mah·lehs·tahr ehs·toh·mah·kahl

Basic Supplies

I'd like...	**Quiero...** *keeyeh·roh...*
acetaminophen	**paracetamol**
[paracetamol]	*pah·rah·seh·tah·mohl*
antiseptic cream	**pomada antiséptica**
	poh·mah·dahahn·tee·sehp·tee·kah
aspirin	**aspirinas** *ahs·pee·ree·nahs*
bandages	**curitas** *koo·ree·tahs*
a comb	**un peine** *oon peyee·neh*
condoms	**condones** *kohn·doh·nehs*
contact lens	**líquido para lentes de contacto**
solution	*lee·kee·doh pah·rah lehn·tehs deh kohn·tahk·toh*
deodorant	**desodorante**
	deh·soh·doh·rahn·teh
a hairbrush	**un cepillo para el pelo**
	oon seh·pee·yoh pah·rah ehl peh·loh
hairspray	**fijador de cabello**
	fee·hah·dohr deh cah·beh·yoh
ibuprofen	**ibuprofeno** *ee·boo·proh·feh·noh*
insect repellent	**repelente de insectos**
	rreh·peh·lehn·tehdeh een·sehk·tohs
lotion	**crema hidratante**
	kreh·mah ee·drah·tahn·teh
a nail file	**una lima de uñas** *oonah lee·mah deh oo·nyahs*

a (disposable) razor	**una navaja de afeitar**	*oo•nah nah•bah•khah deh ah•fehee•tahr*
razor blades	**hojas de afeitar**	*oh•khahs deh ah•feyeé•tahr*
sanitary napkins [pads]	**toallas sanitarias**	*toh•ah•yassah•nee•tah•reeyahs*
shampoo/ conditioner	**champú/acondicionador**	*chahm•poo/ ah•kohn•dee•seeyoh•nah•dohr*
soap	**jabón** *khah•bohn*	
sunscreen	**protector solar**	*proh•tehk•tohr soh•lahr*
tampons	**tampones**	*tahm•poh•nehs*
tissues	**pañuelos desechables**	*pah•nyweh•lohs deh•seh•chah•blehs*
toilet paper	**papel higiénico**	*pah•pehl ee•kheeyeh•nee•koh*
toothpaste	**pasta de dientes**	*pahs•tah deh deeyehn•tehs*

For Baby Essentials, see page 144.

The Basics

Grammar

In Mexican Spanish, there are a number of forms for 'you' (taking different verb forms): tú (singular) is informal, and used when talking to relatives, close friends and children; usted (singular) is used in all other cases. The plural ustedes is both formal and informal. If in doubt, use usted for 'you'. The following abbreviations are used in this section: Ud. = Usted; Uds. = Ustedes.

Regular Verbs

There are three verb types that follow a regular conjugation pattern. These verbs end in **ar**, **er** and **ir**. Following are the present, past and future forms of the verbs **hablar** (to speak), **comer** (to eat) and **vivir** (to live). The different conjugation endings are in bold.

HABLAR		Present	Past	Future
I	**yo**	habl**o**	habl**é**	hablar**é**
you (sing.)	**tú**	habl**as**	habl**aste**	hablar**ás**
he/she/you (for.)	**él/ella/Ud.**	habl**a**	habl**ó**	hablar**á**
we	**nosotros**	habl**amos**	habl**amos**	hablar**emos**
they/you (pl.)	**ellos** m / **ellas** f /**Uds.**	habl**an**	habl**aron**	hablar**án**

COMER		Present	Past	Future
I	**yo**	com**o**	com**í**	comer**é**
you (sing.)	**tú**	com**es**	com**iste**	comer**ás**
he/she/you (for.)	**él/ella/Ud.**	com**e**	com**ió**	comer**á**
we	**nosotros**	com**emos**	com**imos**	comer**emos**
they/you (pl.)	**ellos** m / **ellas** f /**Uds.**	com**en**	com**ieron**	comer**án**

VIVIR		Present	Past	Future
I	**yo**	viv**o**	viv**í**	viv**iré**
you (sing.)	**tú**	viv**es**	viv**iste**	viv**irás**
he/she/you (for.)	**él/ella/Ud.**	viv**e**	viv**ió**	viv**irá**
we	**nosotros**	viv**imos**	viv**imos**	viv**iremos**
they/you (pl.)	**ellos** m / **ellas** f /Uds.	viv**en**	viv**ieron**	viv**irán**

Irregular Verbs

The two most commonly used, and confused, irregular verbs are **ser** and **estar**. Both verbs mean 'to be'.

Ser is used to describe a fixed quality or characteristic. It is also used to tell time and dates.

Example: Yo soy estadounidense. I am American.

Here **ser** is used because it is a permanent characteristic.

Estar is used when describing a physical location or a temporary condition.

Example: Estoy cansado. I am tired.

Here **estar** is used because being tired is a temporary condition.

SER	Present	Past	Future
yo	soy	fui	seré
tú	eres	fuiste	serás
él/ella/Ud.	es	fue	será
nosotros	somos	fuimos	seremos
ellos/ellas/Uds.	son	fueron	serán

ESTAR	Present	Past	Future
yo	estoy	estuve	estaré
tú	estás	estuviste	estarás
él/ella/Ud.	está	estuvo	estará
nosotros	estamos	estuvimos	estaremos
ellos/ellas/Uds.	están	estuvieron	estarán

Nouns & Articles

Nouns are either masculine or feminine. Masculine nouns usually end in **o**, and feminine nouns usually end in **a**. Nouns become plural by adding an **s**, or **es** to nouns not ending in **o** or **a** (e.g. **tren** becomes **trenes**).

Nouns in Spanish take an indefinite (a, an or some) or definite (the) article. An article must agree with the noun to which it refers in gender and number.

Indefinite examples: un tren *m* (a train); **unos trenes** *m* (some trains); **una mesa** *f* (a table); **unas mesas** *f* (some tables)

Definite examples: el libro *m* (the book); **los libros** *m* (the books); **la casa** *f* (the house); **las casas** *f* (the houses)

Word Order

In Spanish, the conjugated verb comes after the subject.

Example: Yo trabajo en Guadalajara. I work in Guadalajara.

To ask a question, reverse the order of the subject and verb, change your intonation or use key question words such as **cuándo** (when).

Examples: ¿Cuándo cierra el banco? When does the bank close?

Literally translates to: "When closes the bank?" Notice the order of the subject and verb is reversed; a question word also begins the sentence.

¿El hotel es viejo? Is the hotel old?

Literally: The hotel is old? This is a statement that becomes a question by raising the pitch of the last syllable of the sentence.

Negation

To form a negative sentence, add **no** (not) before the verb.

Example: Fumamos. We smoke.

No fumamos. We don't smoke.

Imperatives

Imperative sentences, or sentences that are commands, are formed by adding the appropriate ending to the stem of the verb (i.e. the verb in the infinitive without the **-ar**, **-er**, **-ir** ending). Example: Speak!

you (sing.) (inf.)	**tú**	**¡Habla!**
you (sing.) (for.)	**Ud.**	**¡Hable!**
we	**nosotros**	**¡Hablemos!**
you (pl.) (for.)	**Uds.**	**¡Hablen!**

Comparative & Superlative

The comparative is usually formed by adding **más** (more) or **menos** (less)
before the adjective or noun. The superlative is formed by adding the
appropriate definite article (**la/las, el/los**) and **más** (the most) or **menos** (the
least) before the adjective or noun. Example:

grande	**más grande**	**el m /la f más grande**
big	bigger	biggest
caro m /**cara** f	**menos caro**	**el** m /**la** f
	m /**cara** f	**menos caro** m /**cara** f
expensive	less expensive	least expensive

Possessive Pronouns

Pronouns serve as substitutes for specific nouns and must agree with the noun
in gender and number.

	Singular	Plural
mine	**mío** m /**mía** f	**míos** m /**mías** f
yours (inf.)	**tuyo** m /**tuya** f	**tuyos** m /**tuyas** f
yours (for.)	**suyo** m /**suya** f	**suyos** m /**suyas** f
his/her/its	**suyo** m /**suya** f	**suyos** m /**suyas** f
ours	**nuestro** m /**nuestra** f	**nuestros** m /**nuestras** f
theirs	**suyo** m /**suya** f	**suyos** m /**suyas** f

Example: Ese asiento es mío. That seat is mine.

Possessive Adjectives

A possessive adjective must agree in number and gender with the noun that follows.

	Singular	Plural
my	**mi**	**mis**
your (inf.)	**tu**	**tus**
his/her/its	**su**	**sus**
our	**nuestro** m /**nuestra** f	**nuestros** m /**nuestras** f
their/your (for.)	**su**	**sus**

Examples: ¿Dónde está su chamarra? Where is your jacket?
Tu vuelo sale a las ocho. Your flight leaves at eight.

Adjectives

Adjectives describe nouns and must agree with the noun in gender and number. In Spanish, adjectives usually come after the noun. Masculine adjectives generally end in **o**, feminine adjectives in **a**. If the masculine form ends in **e** or with a consonant, the feminine form is generally the same. Most adjectives form their plurals the same way as nouns.

Example: Su hijo/hija es simpático m /**simpática** f.
Your son/daughter is nice.

Adverbs & Adverbial Expressions

Some adverbs are formed by adding -**mente** to the end of the adjective.
Example: Roberto conduce lentamente. Robert drives slowly.
The following are some common adverbial time expressions:

actualmente	currently
todavía	no not yet
todavía	still
ya no	not anymore

Numbers

ESSENTIAL

0	**cero**	seh·roh
1	**uno**	oo·noh
2	**dos**	dohs
3	**tres**	trehs
4	**cuatro**	kwah·troh
5	**cinco**	seen·koh
6	**seis**	seyees
7	**siete**	seeyeh·teh
8	**ocho**	oh·choh
9	**nueve**	nweh·beh
10	**diez**	deeyehs
11	**once**	ohn·seh
12	**doce**	doh·seh
13	**trece**	treh·seh
14	**catorce**	kah·tohr·seh
15	**quince**	keen·seh
16	**dieciséis**	deeyeh·see·seyees
17	**diecisiete**	deeyeh·see·seeyeh·teh
18	**dieciocho**	deeyeh·see·oh·choh
19	**diecinueve**	deeyeh·see·nweh·beh
20	**veinte**	beyeen·teh
21	**veintiuno**	beyeen·tee·oo·noh
22	**veintidós**	beyeen·tee·dohs
30	**treinta**	treyeen·tah
31	**treinta y uno**	treyeen·tah ee oo·noh
40	**cuarenta**	kwah·rehn·tah
50	**cincuenta**	seen·kwehn·tah

60	**sesenta** seh·sehn·tah
70	**setenta** seh·tehn·tah
80	**ochenta** oh·chehn·tah
90	**noventa** noh·behn·tah
100	**cien** seeyehn
101	**ciento uno** seeyehn·toh oo·noh
200	**doscientos** dohs·seeyehn·tohs
500	**quinientos** kee·neeyehn·tohs
1,000	**mil** meel
10,000	**diez mil** deeyehs meel
1,000,000	**un millón** oon mee·yohn

Ordinal Numbers

first	**primero** m /**primera** f
	pree·meh·roh m /pree·meh·rah f
second	**segundo** m /**segunda** f
	seh·goon·doh m /seh·goon·dah f
third	**tercero** m /**tercera** f
	tehr·seh·roh m /tehr·seh·rah f
fourth	**cuarto** m /**cuarta** f kwahr·toh m /kwahr·tah f
fifth	**quinto** m /**quinta** f keen·toh m /keen·tah f
once	**una vez** oo·nah behs
twice	**dos veces** dohs beh·ses
three times	**tres veces** trehs beh·ses

In Mexico you use the greeting **Buenos días** until lunch time (about 2:00p.m.). After 2:00p.m., you should use **Buenos tardes** (good afternoon/evening) until it gets dark. **Buenas noches** is then used. It also means good night.

Time

ESSENTIAL

What time is it?	**¿Qué hora es?** *keh oh•rah ehs*
It's midday.	**Son las doce del día.** *sohn lahs doh•seh dehl dee•ah*
At midnight.	**A medianoche.** *ah meh•deeyah•noh•cheh*
From one o'clock to two o'clock.	**De una a dos en punto.** *deh oo•nah ah dohs ehn poon•toh*
Five past three.	**Las tres y cinco.** *lahs trehs ee seen•koh*
A quarter to five.	**Cuarto para las cinco.** *kwahr•toh pah•rah lahs seen•koh*
5:30 a.m./p.m.	**Las cinco y media de la mañana/tarde.** *lahs seen•koh ee meh•deeyah deh lah mah•nyah•nah/tahr•deh*

Days

ESSENTIAL

Monday	**lunes** *loo•nehs*
Tuesday	**martes** *mahr•tehs*
Wednesday	**miércoles** *meeyehr•koh•lehs*
Thursday	**jueves** *khweh•behs*
Friday	**viernes** *beeyehr•nehs*
Saturday	**sábado** *sah•bah•doh*
Sunday	**domingo** *doh•meen•goh*

Dates

yesterday	**ayer** *ah·yehr*
today	**hoy** *oy*
tomorrow	**mañana** *mah·nyah·nah*
day	**día** *dee·ah*
week	**semana** *seh·mah·nah*
month	**mes** *mehs*
year	**año** *ah·nyoh*

Dates follow a day-month-year format in Mexico:
el uno de marzo de 2014 = March 1, 2014 = 1.3.14 = 3/1/2014

Months

January	**enero** *eh·neh·roh*
February	**febrero** *feh·breh·roh*
March	**marzo** *mahr·soh*
April	**abril** *ah·breel*
May	**mayo** *mah·yoh*
June	**junio** *khoo·neeyoh*
July	**julio** *khoo·leeyoh*
August	**agosto** *ah·gohs·toh*
September	**septiembre** *sehp·teeyehm·breh*
October	**octubre** *ohk·too·breh*
November	**noviembre** *noh·beeyehm·breh*
December	**diciembre** *dee·seeyehm·breh*

Seasons

spring	**la primavera** *lah pree·mah·beh·rah*
summer	**el verano** *ehl beh·rah·noh*
autumn	**el otoño** *ehl oh·toh·nyoh*
winter	**el invierno** *ehl een·beeyehr·noh*

Holidays

January 1: New Year's Day	**Año Nuevo**	
February 5: Constitution Day,	**Día de la Constitución**	
March 21: Benito Juarez Day,	**Natalicio de Benito Juarez**	
May 1: Labor Day	**Día del Trabajo**	
September 16: Independence Day	**Día de la Independencia**	
November 1: All Saint's Day,	**Fieles Difuntos**	
November 20: Mexican Revolution's Day,	**Día de la Revolución Mexicana**	
December 12: Feast of the Virgin of Guadalupe	**Día de la Virgen de Guadalupe**	
December 25: Christmas	**Navidad**	
Moveable Dates		
Easter	**Pascua**	

Conversion Tables

When you know	Multiply by	To find
ounces	28.3	grams
pounds	0.45	kilograms
inches	2.54	centimeters
feet	0.3	meters
miles	1.61	kilometers
square inches	6.45	sq. centimeters
square feet	0.09	sq. meters
square miles	2.59	sq. kilometers
pints (U.S./Brit)	0.47/0.56	liters
gallons (U.S./Brit)	3.8/4.5	liters
Fahrenheit	-32, / 1.8	Centigrade
Centigrade	+32, x 1.8	Fahrenheit

Kilometers to Miles Conversions

1 km	= 0.62 miles	**20 km**	= 12.4 miles
5 km	= 3.1 miles	**50 km**	= 31 miles
10 km	= 6.20 miles	**100 km**	= 62 miles

Measurement

1 gram	= **1000 milligrams**	= 0.035 oz.
1 kilogram (kg)	= **1000 grams**	= 2.2 lb
1 liter (l)	= **1000 milliliters**	= 1.06 U.S./0.88
1 centimeter	= **10 millimeters**	= 0.4 inch (cm)
1 meter (m)	= **100 centimeters**	= 39.37 inches/ 3.28 ft.
1 kilometer	= **1000 meters**	= 0.62 mile (km)

Temperature

-40°C = -40°F	**-1°C** = 30°F	**20°C** = 68°F
-30°C = -22°F	**0°C** = 32°F	**25°C** = 77°F
-20°C = -4°F	**5°C** = 41°F	**30°C** = 86°F
-10°C = 14°F	**10°C** = 50°F	**35°C** = 95°F
-5°C = 23°F	**15°C** = 59°F	

Oven Temperature

100° C = 212° F	**177° C** = 350° F
121° C = 250° F	**204° C** = 400° F
149° C = 300° F	**260° C** = 500° F

Dictionary

English–Mexican Spanish 174
Mexican Spanish–English 200

cancel v cancelar
candy el caramelo
canned goods las conservas
nyon el cañón
el auto; ~ hire [BE]
enta de autos;
rk [BE] el estacionamiento;
tal el alquiler de autos;
el asiento de niño
jarra
rjeta; ATM ~ la tarjeta de
omático;
tarjeta de crédito;
rjeta de débito;
rjeta de teléfono
of hand
uipaje de

canadiense
relatas   el

Celsius el grad
centimeter el cer
certificate el cer
chair la silla
change v (buses)
~ n (money) el ca
charcoal el carbón
charge v (credit car
~ n (cost) el precio
cheap barato
check v (on something
~ v (luggage) registra
~ n (payment) registra
~-in (airport) el chequ
~-in (hotel) la docume
~ing account el registro;
corriente; ~-out (hotel) la cuenta
Cheers! ¡Salud!
chemical toilet el excusa
químico
chemist [B]

A

abbey *la abadía*
accept *v aceptar*
access *el acceso*
accident *el accidente*
accommodation
  el alojamiento
account *la cuenta*
acupuncture *la acupuntura*
adapter *el adaptador*
address *la dirección*
admission *la entrada*
after *después;*
  ~ noon *la tarde;*
  ~ shave *la loción para después de afeitar*
age *la edad*
agency *la agencia*
AIDS *el sida*
air *el aire;*
  ~ conditioning *el aire acondicionado;*
  ~ line *la aerolínea;*
  ~ mail *el correo aéreo;*
  ~ plane *el avión;*
  ~ port *el aeropuerto*

aisle *el pasillo;*
  ~ seat *el asiento de pasillo*
allergic *alérgico;*
  ~ reaction *la reacción alérgica*
allow *v permitir*
alone *solo*
alter *v* **(clothing)** *hacer un ajuste*
alternate route *el otro camino*
aluminum foil *el papel aluminio*
amazing *increíble*
ambulance *la ambulancia*
American *estadounidense*
amusement park *el parque de diversiones*
anemic *anémico*
anesthesia *la anestesia*
animal *el animal*
ankle *el tobillo*
antibiotic *el antibiótico*
antiques store *la tienda de -antigüedades*
antiseptic cream *la pomada antiséptica*
anything *algo*
apartment *el departamento*
appendix (body part) *el apéndice*

adj adjective	**BE** British English	**prep** preposition
adv adverb	**n** noun	**v** verb

appetizer *el aperitivo*
appointment *la cita*
arcade *el salón de juegos de video*
area code *el código de área*
arm *el brazo*
aromatherapy *la aromaterapia*
around (the corner) *doblando (la esquina)*
arrivals (airport) *las llegadas*
arrive *v llegar*
artery *la arteria*
arthritis *la artritis*
arts *las letras*
aspirin *la aspirina*
asthmatic *asmático*
ATM *el cajero automático*
attack *la agresión*
attend *v asistir*
attraction (place) *el sitio de interés*
attractive *guapo*
Australia *Australia*
Australian *australiano*
automatic *automático;*
  ~ car *auto automático*
available *disponible*

B

baby *el bebé;*
  ~ bottle *el biberón;*
  ~ wipe *la toallita;*
  ~ sitter *la niñera*

back *la espalda;*
  ~ ache *el dolor de espalda;*
  ~ pack *la mochila*
bag *la maleta*
baggage *el equipaje;*
  ~ claim *el reclamo de equipaje;*
  ~ ticket *el talón de equipaje*
bakery *la panadería*
ballet *el ballet*
bandage *la curita*
bank *el banco*
bar *el antro*
barbecue *la parrillada*
barber *la peluquería*
baseball *el béisbol*
basket (grocery store) *la canasta*
basketball *el básquetbol*
bathroom *el baño*
battery *la pila*
battery (car) *la batería*
battleground *el campo de batalla*
be *v ser/estar*
beach *la playa*
beautiful *bello*
bed *la cama;*
  ~ and breakfast *la pensión*
before *antes de*
begin *v empezar*
beginner *principiante*
behind *detrás de*
beige *beige*

belt *el cinturón*
berth *la litera*
best *mejor*
better *mejor*
bicycle *la bicicleta*
big *grande*
bigger *más grande*
bike route *la ruta para bicicletas*
bikini *el bikini;*
  ~ wax *la depilación de las ingles*
bill *v* **(charge)** *cobrar;*
  ~ *n* **(money)** *el billete;*
  ~ *n* **(of sale)** *el recibo*
bird *el pájaro*
birthday *el cumpleaños*
black *negro*
bladder *la vejiga*
bland *insípido*
blanket *la cobija*
bleed *v sangrar*
blood *la sangre;*
  ~ pressure *la presión arterial*
blouse *la blusa*
board *v embarcar*
boarding pass *el pase de abordar*
boat *el barco*
bone *el hueso*
book *el libro;*
  ~store *la librería*
boots *las botas*
boring *aburrido*

botanical garden
  el jardín botánico
bother *v molestar*
bottle *la botella;*
  ~ opener *el destapador*
bowl *el tazón*
box *la caja*
boxing match *la pelea de boxeo*
boy *el niño;*
  ~ friend *el novio*
bra *el sostén*
bracelet *la pulsera*
brakes (car) *los frenos*
break *v romper*
break-in (burglary)
  el allanamiento de morada
breakdown *la avería*
breakfast *el desayuno*
breast *el seno;* **~feed** *dar pecho*
breathe *v respirar*
bridge *el puente*
briefs (clothing) *los calzones*
bring *v traer*
British *británico*
broken *roto*
brooch *el broche*
broom *la escoba*
brother *el hermano*
bug *el insecto*
building *el edificio*
burn *v quemar*

bus *el camión;*
  ~ station *la estación de camiones;*
  ~ stop *la parada de camiones;*
  ~ ticket *el boleto del camión;*
  ~ tour *el recorrido en camión*
business *los negocios;*
  ~ card *la tarjeta de presentación;*
  ~ center *el centro de negocios;*
  ~ class *la clase ejecutiva;*
  ~ hours *el horario de atención al público*
butcher *el carnicero*
buttocks *los gluteos*
buy *v comprar*
bye *adiós*

C

cabin (house) *la cabaña;*
  ~ (ship) *el camarote*
cable car *el teleférico*
cafe *la cafetería*
call *v llamar;* **~***n la llamada*
calories *las calorías*
camera *la cámara;*
  ~ case *el estuche para la cámara;*
  ~ store *la tienda de fotografía;*
  digital ~ *la cámara digital*
camp *v acampar;*
  ~ site *el campamento*
can opener *el abrelatas*
Canada *Canadá*
Canadian *canadiense*

cancel *v cancelar*
candy *el caramelo*
canned goods *las conservas*
canyon *el cañón*
car *el auto;*
  ~ hire [BE] *la renta de autos;*
  ~ park [BE] *el estacionamiento;*
  ~ rental *el alquiler de autos;*
  ~ seat *el asiento de niño*
carafe *la jarra*
card *la tarjeta;* **ATM ~** *la tarjeta de cajero automático;*
  credit ~ *la tarjeta de crédito;*
  debit ~ *la tarjeta de débito;*
  phone ~ *la tarjeta de teléfono*
carry-on (piece of hand luggage) *el equipaje de mano*
cart (grocery store) *el carrito;*
  ~ (luggage) *el carrito para el equipaje*
carton *el cartón;*
  ~ of cigarettes *la cajetilla de cigarros*
case (amount) *la caja*
cash *v cobrar;*
  ~*n el efectivo;*
  ~ advance *sacar dinero de la tarjeta*
cashier *el cajero*
castle *el castillo*
cathedral *la catedral*

cave *la cueva*

CD *el CD*

cell phone *el teléfono celular*

Celsius *el grado centígrado*

centimeter *el centímetro*

certificate *el certificado*

chair *la silla*

change *v* **(buses)** *transbordar;*
~ *n* **(money)** *el cambio*

charcoal *el carbón*

charge *v* **(credit card)** *cobrar;*
~ *n* **(cost)** *el precio*

cheap *barato*

check *v* **(on something)** *revisar;*
~ *v* **(luggage)** *registrar;*
~ *n* **(payment)** *el cheque;*
~ **-in (airport)** *la documentación;*
~ **-in (hotel)** *el registro;*
~ **ing account** *la cuenta corriente;*
~ **-out (hotel)** *la salida*

Cheers! *¡Salud!*

chemical toilet *el excusado químico*

chemist [BE] *la farmacia*

cheque [BE] *el cheque*

chest (body part) *el pecho;*
~ **pain** *el dolor de pecho*

chewing gum *el chicle*

child *el niño;*
~ **seat** *la silla para niños*

children's menu *el menú para niños*

children's portion *la ración para niños*

church *la iglesia*

cigar *el puro*

cigarette *el cigarrillo*

class *la clase;*

business ~ *la clase ejecutiva;*

economy ~ *la clase turista;*

first ~ *la primera clase*

classical music *la música clásica*

clean *v limpiar;*
~ *adj limpio;*
~ **ing product** *el producto de limpieza;*
~ **ing supplies** *los productos de limpieza*

clear v (on an ATM) *borrar*

cliff *el acantilado*

cling film [BE] *el plástico transparente*

close *v* **(a shop)** *cerrar*

closed *cerrado*

clothing *la ropa;*
~ **store** *la tienda de ropa*

club *la discoteca*

coat *el abrigo*

coffee shop *la cafetería*

coin *la moneda*

colander *el colador*

cold *n* **(sickness)** *el resfriado;*
~ *adj* **(temperature)** *frío*

colleague *el compañero de trabajo*

cologne *la colonia*

color *el color*

comb *el peine*

come *v venir*

complaint *la queja*

computer *la computadora*

concert *el concierto;*
  ~ hall *la sala de conciertos*

condition (medical)
  el problema de salud

conditioner *el acondicionador*

condom *el condón*

conference *la conferencia*

confirm *v confirmar*

congestion *la congestión*

connect *v* **(internet)** *conectarse*

connection (internet) *la conexión;*
  ~ (flight) *la conexión de vuelo*

constipated *estreñido*

consulate *el consulado*

consultant *el consultor*

contact *v ponerse en contacto con*

contact lens *el lente de contacto;*
  ~ solution *el líquido para lentes de contacto*

contagious *contagioso*

convention hall *el centro de congresos*

conveyor belt *la cinta transportadora*

cook *v cocinar*

cooking gas *el gas butano*

cool (temperature) *frío*

copper *el cobre*

corkscrew *el sacacorchos*

cost *v costar*

cot *el catre*

cotton *el algodón*

cough *v toser;*
  ~ n *la tos*

country code *el código de país*

cover charge *el cover*

crash v (car) *estrellarse*

cream (ointment) *la pomada*

credit card *la tarjeta de crédito*

crew neck *el cuello redondo*

crib *la cuna*

crystal *el cristal*

cup *la taza*

currency *la moneda;*
  ~ exchange
  el cambio de divisas;
  ~ exchange office *la casa de cambio*

current account [BE]
  la cuenta de cheques

customs *las aduanas*

cut v (hair) *cortar;*
  ~ n (injury) *el corte*

cute *bonito*

cycling *el ciclismo*

D

damage v causar daño
damaged ha sufrido daños
dance v bailar;
~ **club** la discoteca
dangerous peligroso
dark oscuro
date (calendar) la fecha
day el día
deaf sordo
debit card la tarjeta de débito
deck chair el camastro
declare v declarar
decline v (credit card) rechazar
deep hondo
degrees (temperature) los grados
delay v retrasar
delete v (computer) borrar
delicatessen la salchichonería
delicious delicioso
denim la mezclilla
dentist el dentista
denture la dentadura
deodorant el desodorante
department store las tiendas
  departamentales
departures (airport) las salidas
deposit v depositar;
~ n **(bank)** el depósito bancario;
~ n **(reserve a room)** el depósito
desert el desierto

dessert el postre
detergent el detergente
develop v (film) revelar
diabetic diabético
dial v marcar
diamond el diamante
diaper el pañal
diarrhea la diarrea
diesel el diésel
difficult difícil
digital digital;
~ **camera** la cámara digital;
~ **photos** las fotos digitales;
~ **prints** las fotos digitales
dining room el comedor
dinner la cena
direction la dirección
dirty sucio
disabled discapacitado
disconnect (computer)
  desconectar
discount el descuento
dish (kitchen) el plato;
~ **washer** el lavaplatos;
~ **washing liquid** el líquido
  lavaplatos
display v mostrar;
~ **case** la vitrina
disposable desechable;
~ **razor** la cuchilla desechable
dive v bucear

diving equipment *el equipo de buceo*

divorce *v divorciar*

dizzy *mareado*

doctor *el doctor*

doll *la muñeca*

dollar (U.S.) *el dólar*

domestic *nacional;*
  ~ flight *el vuelo nacional*

door *la puerta*

dormitory *el dormitorio*

double bed *la cama matrimonial*

downtown *el centro*

dozen *la docena*

dress (piece of clothing) *el vestido;*
  ~ code *las normas de vestimenta*

drink *v beber;*
  ~ *n la bebida;*
  ~ menu *la carta de bebidas;*
  ~ing water *el agua potable*

drive *v conducir*

driver's license number
  licencia de conducir

drop (medicine) *la gota*

drowsiness *la somnolencia*

dry cleaner *la tintorería*

dubbed *doblado*

during *durante*

duty (tax) *el impuesto;*
  ~-free *libre de impuestos*

DVD *el DVD*

E

ear *la oreja;* **~ache** *el dolor de oído*

early *temprano*

earrings *los aretes*

east *el este*

easy *fácil*

eat *v comer*

economy class *la clase turista*

elbow *el codo*

electric outlet *el enchufe*

elevator *el elevador*

e-mail *v enviar un correo electrónico;*
  ~ *n el correo electrónico;*
  ~ address *la dirección de correo electrónico*

emergency *la urgencia;*
  ~ exit *la salida de emergencia*

empty *v vaciar*

enamel (jewelry) *el esmalte*

end *v terminar*

English *el inglés*

engrave *v grabar*

enjoy *v disfrutar*

enter *v entrar*

entertainment *el entretenimiento*

entrance *la entrada*

envelope *el sobre*

equipment *el equipo*

escalators *las escaleras eléctricas*

e-ticket *el boleto electrónico*

evening *la noche*

excess *el exceso*
exchange *v* **(money)** *cambiar;*
~ *v* **(goods)** *devolver;*
~ *n* **(place)** *la casa de cambio;*
~ **rate** *el tipo de cambio*
excursion *la excursión*
excuse *v* **(to get past)** *pedir perdón;*
~ *v* **(to get attention)** *disculparse*
exhausted *agotado*
exit *v* *salir;*
~ *n* *la salida*
expensive *caro*
expert (skill level) *experto*
exposure (film) *la foto*
express *rápido;*
~ **bus** *el camión rápido;*
~ **train** *el tren rápido*
extension (phone) *la extensión*
extra *adicional;*
~ **large** *extra grande*
extract *v* **(tooth)** *extraer*
eye *el ojo*
eyebrow wax *la depilación de cejas*

F

face *la cara*
facial *el facial*
family *la familia*
fan (appliance) *el ventilador;*
~ **(souvenir)** *el abanico*

far *lejos;*
~**-sighted** *hipermétrope*
farm *la granja*
fast *rápido;*
~ **food** *la comida rápida*
father *el padre*
fax *v* *enviar un fax;*
~ *n* *el fax;*
~ **number** *el número de fax*
fee *la tarifa*
feed *v* *alimentar*
ferry *el transbordador*
fever *la fiebre*
field (sports) *la cancha*
fill *v* *llenar ;* ~ **out** *v* **(form)** *llenar*
filling (tooth) *la tapadura*
film (camera) *el rollo*
fine (fee for breaking law) *la multa*
finger *el dedo;*
~ **nail** *la uña*
fire *fuego;*
~ **department** *los bomberos;*
~ **door** *la puerta de incendios*
first *primero;*
~ **class** *la primera clase*
fit (clothing) *queda bien*
fitting room *el probador*
fix *v* **(repair)** *reparar*
flashlight *la linterna*

flight *el vuelo*

floor *el suelo*

flower *la flor*

folk music *la música folclórica*

food *la comida*

foot *el pie*

football [BE] *el fútbol*

for *para/por*

forecast *el pronóstico*

forest *el bosque*

fork *el tenedor*

form *el formulario*

formula (baby) *la fórmula*

fort *el fuerte*

fountain *la fuente*

free *gratuito*

freezer *el congelador*

fresh *fresco*

friend *el amigo*

frying pan *el sartén*

full *completo;*
~**-service** *el servicio completo;*
~**-time** *de tiempo completo*

G

game *el partido*

garage (parking) *el garaje;*
~ **(repair)** *el taller*

garbage bag *la bolsa de basura*

gas *la gasolina;*
~ **station** *la gasolinera*

gate (airport) *la puerta*

gay *gay;*
~ **bar** *el antro gay;*
~ **club** *la discoteca gay*

gel (hair) *el gel*

get off *v* **(a train/bus/subway)**
bajarse

get to *v ir a*

gift *el regalo;*
~ **shop** *la tienda de regalos*

girl *la niña;*
~ **friend** *la novia*

give *v dar*

glass (drinking) *el vaso;*
~ **(material)** *el vidrio*

glasses *los anteojos*

go *v* **(somewhere)** *ir a*

gold *el oro*

golf *golf;*
~ **course** *el campo de golf;*
~ **tournament**
el torneo de golf

good *n el producto;*
~ *adj bueno;*
~ **afternoon** *buenas tardes;*
~ **evening** *buenas noches;*
~ **morning** *buenos días;*
~ **bye** *adiós*

gram *el gramo*

grandchild *el nieto*

grandparents *los abuelos*

grocery store *el supermercado*

ground *la tierra;*
~ **floor** *la planta baja;*
~**cloth** *la tela impermeable*
group *el grupo*
guide *el guía;*
~ **book** *la guía;*
~ **dog** *el perro guía*
gym *el gimnasio*
gynecologist *el ginecólogo*

H

hair *el pelo;*
~ **dryer** *el secador de pelo;*
~ **salon** *el salón de belleza;*
~ **stylist** *el estilista;*
~ **brush** *el cepillo de pelo;*
~ **cut** *el corte de pelo;*
~ **spray** *la laca;*
~ **style** *el peinado*
half *medio;*
~ **hour** *la media hora;*
~ **kilo** *el medio kilo*
hammer *el martillo*
hand *la mano;*
~ **luggage [BE]** *el equipaje de mano*
~ **bag [BE]** *el bolso;*
handicapped *discapacitado*
hangover *la cruda*
happy *feliz*
hat *el sombrero*
have *v tener*

head (body part) *la cabeza;*
~ **ache** *el dolor de cabeza;*
~ **phones** *los audífonos*
health *la salud;*
~ **food store** *la tienda de alimentos naturales*
heart *el corazón;*
~ **condition** *padecer del corazón*
heat *v calentar;*
~*n el calor*
heater *la calefacción*
hello *hola*
helmet *el casco*
help *v ayudar;*
~*n la ayuda*
here *aquí*
hi *hola*
high *alto;*
~ **chair** *la periquera;*
~ **way** *la autopista*
hiking boots *las botas de excursionista*
hill *la colina*
hire v [BE] *alquilar;*
~ **car [BE]** *el coche de alquiler*
hitchhike *pedir aventón*
hockey *el hockey*
holiday [BE] *las vacaciones*
horse track *el hipódromo*
hospital *el hospital*
hostel *el hostal*

hot (temperature) *caliente;*
~ **(spicy)** *picante;*
~ **spring** *el agua termal;*
~ **water** *el agua caliente*
hotel *el hotel*
hour *la hora*
house *la casa;*
~ **hold goods** *los artículos para el hogar;*
~ **keeping services** *el servicio de limpieza de habitaciones*
how (question) *cómo;*
~ **much (question)** *cuánto cuesta*
hug *v abrazar*
hungry *hambriento*
hurt *v* **(have pain)** *tener dolor*
husband *el esposo*

I

ibuprofen *el ibuprofeno*
ice *el hielo;*
~ **hockey** *el hockey sobre hielo*
icy *helado*
identification *la identificación*
ill *v* **(to feel)** *sentirse mal*
in *dentro*
include *v incluir*
indoor pool *la alberca cubierta*
inexpensive *barato*
infected *infectado*
information (phone) *el número de teléfono de información;*

~ **desk** *el módulo de información*
insect *el insecto;*
~ **bite** *el piquete de insecto;*
~ **repellent** *el repelente de insectos*
insert *v introducir*
insomnia *el insomnio*
instant message *el mensaje instantáneo*
insulin *la insulina*
insurance *el seguro;*
~ **card** *la credencial de seguro;*
~ **company** *la compañía de seguros*
interesting *interesante*
intermediate *el nivel intermedio*
international (airport area) *internacional;*
~ **flight** *el vuelo internacional;*
~ **student card** *la credencial internacional de estudiante*
internet *el Internet;*
~ **cafe** *el café Internet;*
~ **service** *el servicio de Internet;*
wireless ~ *el acceso inalámbrico*
interpreter *intérprete*
intersection *el cruce*
intestine *el intestino*
introduce *v presentar*
invoice [BE] *la factura*

Ireland *Irlanda*
Irish *irlandés*
iron *n la plancha;*
  ~ *v* **(clothes)** *planchar*

J

jacket *la chamarra*
jar *el bote*
jaw *la mandíbula*
jazz *el jazz;*
  ~ **club** *el club de jazz*
jeans *los jeans*
jet ski *la moto acuática*
jeweler's *la joyería*
jewelry *las joyas*
join *v acompañar a*
joint (body part)
  la articulación

K

key *la llave;*
  ~ **card** *la llave electrónica;*
  ~ **ring** *el llavero*
kiddie pool *el chapoteadero*
kidney (body part) *el riñón*
kilo *el kilo;*
  ~**gram** *el kilogramo;*
  ~**meter** *el kilómetro*
kiss *v besar*
kitchen *la cocina;*
  ~ **foil [BE]** *el papel aluminio*
knee *la rodilla*
knife *el cuchillo*

L

lace *el encaje*
lactose intolerant *intolerante a la lactosa*
lake *el lago*
large *grande*
last *último*
late (time) *tarde*
laundrette [BE] *la lavandería*
laundromat *la lavandería*
laundry *lavar ropa;*
  ~ **service** *el servicio de lavandería*
lawyer *el abogado*
leather *el cuero*
to leave *v salir*
left (direction) *la izquierda*
leg *la pierna*
lens *el lente*
less *menos*
lesson *la lección*
letter *la carta*
library *la biblioteca*
life *la vida;*
  ~ **jacket** *el chaleco salvavidas;*
  ~**guard** *rescatista*
lift n [BE] *el elevador;*
  ~ *v* **(to give a ride)**
  llevar en auto;
  ~ **pass** *el pase de acceso a los remontes*

light *n* (**overhead**) *la luz;*
~ *v* (**cigarette**) *encender un cigarrillo;*
~**bulb** *el foco*
lighter *el encendedor*
like *v gustar;* **I like** *me gusta*
line (**train**) *la línea*
linen *el lino*
lip *el labio*
liquor store *la licorería*
liter *el litro*
little *chico*
live *v vivir*
liver (**body part**) *el hígado*
loafers *los mocasines*
local *de la zona*
lock *v cerrar;*
~*n el cerrojo*
locker *el casillero*
log off *v* (**computer**) *cerrar sesión*
log on *v* (**computer**) *iniciar sesión*
long *largo;*
~**-sighted** [BE] *hipermétrope;*
~ **sleeves** *las mangas largas;*
look *v mirar*
lose *v* (**something**) *perder*
lost *perdido;*
~ **and found** *la oficina de objetos perdidos*
lotion *la loción*

love *v querer;*
~*n el amor*
low *bajo*
luggage *el equipaje;*
~ **cart** *el carrito de equipaje;*
~ **locker** *el casillero automático;*
~ **ticket** *el talón de equipaje;*
hand ~ [BE] *el equipaje de mano*
lunch *la comida*
lung *el pulmón*

M

magazine *la revista*
magnificent *magnífico*
mail *v enviar por correo;*
~ *n el correo;*
~**box** *el buzón de correo*
main *principal;*
~ **attractions** *los principales sitios de interés;*
~ **course** *el plato principal*
make up a prescription *v* [BE] *surtir medicamentos*
mall *el centro comercial*
man *el hombre*
manager *el gerente*
manicure *el manicure*
manual car *el auto con transmisión manual*
map *el mapa*
market *el mercado*
married *casado*

marry v casarse
mass (church service) la misa
massage el masaje
match el fósforo
meal la comida
measure v (someone) medir
measuring cup la taza medidora
measuring spoon la cuchara
  medidora
mechanic el mecánico
medicine el medicamento
medium (size) mediano
meet v (someone) conocer
meeting la reunión;
  ~ **room** la sala de reuniones
membership card la tarjeta de
  membresía
memorial (place) el monumento
  conmemorativo
memory card la tarjeta de memoria
mend v zurcir
menstrual cramps los cólicos
  menstruales
menu la carta
message el mensaje
meter (parking) el estacionómetro
Mexican mexicano
Mexico México
microwave el microondas
midday [BE] el mediodía
midnight la medianoche

mileage el kilometraje
mini-bar el minibar
minute el minuto
missing perdido
mistake el error
mobile móvil;
  ~ **home** casa rodante;
  ~ **phone [BE]** el teléfono celular
mobility la movilidad
money el dinero
month el mes
mop el trapeador
moped la bicimoto
more más
morning la mañana
mosque la mezquita
mother la madre
motion sickness el mareo
motor el motor;
  ~ **boat** la lancha de motor;
  ~**cycle** la motocicleta;
  ~ **way [BE]** la autopista
mountain la montaña;
  ~ **bike** la bicicleta de montaña
mousse (hair) el mousse para el
  pelo
mouth la boca
movie la película;
  ~ **theater** el cine
mug v asaltar
muscle (body part) el músculo

museum *el museo*

music *la música;*

  ~ store *la tienda de músican*

nail *la uˉna;*

  ~ file *la lima de uñas;*

  ~ salon *el salón de manicure*

name *el nombre*

napkin *la servilleta*

nappy [BE] *el pañal*

nationality *la nacionalidad*

nature preserve *la reserva natural*

(be) nauseous *v tener náuseas*

near *cerca;*

  ~ by *cerca de aquí;*

  ~-sighted *miope*

neck *el cuello*

necklace *el collar*

need *v necesitar*

newspaper *el periódico*

newsstand *el puesto de periódicos*

next *siguiente*

nice *amable*

night *la noche;*

  ~club *la discoteca*

no *no*

non *sin;*

  ~-alcoholic *sin alcohol;*

  ~-smoking *para no fumadores*

noon *el mediodía*

north *el norte*

nose *la nariz*

note [BE] *el billete*

nothing *nada*

notify *v avisar*

novice (skill level) *principiante*

now *ahora*

number *el número*

nurse *el enfermero?/la enfermera/*

O

office *la oficina;*

  ~ hours (doctor's)
  las horas de consulta;

  ~ hours (other offices)
  el horario de oficina

off-licence [BE] *licorería*

oil *el aceite*

OK *de acuerdo*

old *viejo*

on the corner *en la esquina*

once *una vez*

one *un, uno;*

  ~-way ticket *el boleto sencillo*

only *solamente*

open *v abrir;*

  ~adj abierto

opera *la ópera;*

  ~ house *el teatro de la ópera*

opposite *frente a*

optician *el oculista*

orange (color) *naranja*

orchestra *la orquesta*

order *v pedir*

outdoor pool *la alberca exterior*
outside *fuera*
over *sobre;*
  ~ the counter (medication)
  sin receta;
  ~ look (scenic place) *el mirador;*
  ~ night *por la noche*
oxygen treatment *la oxígenoterapia*

P

pacifier *el chupón*
pack *v hacer las maletas*
package *el paquete*
paddling pool [BE] *el chapoteadero*
pad [BE] *la toalla sanitaria*
pain *el dolor*
pajamas *las pijamas*
palace *el palacio*
pants *los pantalones*
pantyhose *las medias*
paper *el papel;*
  ~ towel *toallas de papel*
paracetamol [BE] *el paracetamol*
park *v estacionar;*
  ~ n *el parque;*
  ~ ing garage *el garage;*
  ~ ing lot *el estacionamiento*
parliament building *el palacio de justicia*
part (for car) *la pieza;*
  ~-time *medio tiempo*

pass through *v estar de paso*
passenger *el pasajero*
passport *el pasaporte;*
  ~ control *migración*
password *la contraseña*
pastry shop *la pastelería*
path *el camino*
pay *v pagar;*
  ~ phone *el teléfono público*
peak (of a mountain) *la cima*
pearl *la perla*
pedestrian *el peatón*
pediatrician *el pediatra*
pedicure *el pedicure*
pen *la pluma*
penicillin *la penicilina*
penis *el pene*
per *por;*
  ~ day *por día;*
  ~ hour *por hora;*
  ~ night *por noche;*
  ~ week *por semana*
perfume *el perfume*
period (menstrual) *la regla;*
  ~ (of time) *la época*
permit *v permitir*
personal identification number (PIN) *el número de identificación personal (NIP)*
pesos (Mexican currency) *pesos petite las tallas pequeñas*

petrol [BE] *la gasolina;*
~ **station** [BE] *la gasolinera*
pewter *el pewter*
pharmacy *la farmacia*
phone *v hacer una llamada;*
~ *n el teléfono;*
~ **call** *la llamada de teléfono;*
~ **card** *la tarjeta de teléfono;*
~ **number** *el número de teléfono*
photo *la foto;*
~ **copy** *la fotocopia;*
~ **graphy** *la fotografía*
pick up *v (something) recoger*
picnic area *el área para día de campo*
piece *el trozo*
pill *(birth control) el anticonceptivo*
pillow *la almohada*
piste [BE] *la pista;*
~ **map** [BE] *el mapa de pistas*
pizzeria *la pizzería*
place *v (a bet) hacer una apuesta*
plane *el avión*
plastic wrap *el plástico transparente*
plate *el plato*
platform [BE] *(train) el andén*
platinum *el platino*
play *v jugar;*
~ *n (theater) la obra de teatro;*
~ **ground** *el patio de recreo*

please *por favor*
pleasure *el placer*
plunger *el destapador*
plus size *la talla extra*
pocket *el bolsillo*
poison *el veneno*
police *la policía;*
~ **report** *la denuncia;*
~ **station** *la comisaría*
pond *el estanque*
pool *la alberca*
pop music *la música pop*
portion *la porción*
post [BE] *el correo;*
~ **office** *la oficina de correos;*
~ **box** [BE] *el buzón de correos;*
~ **card** *la postal*
pot *la olla*
pottery *la cerámica*
pounds *(British sterling) las libras esterlinas*
pregnant *embarazada*
prescribe *v recetar*
prescription *la receta*
press *v (clothing) planchar*
price *el precio*
print *v imprimir*
problem *el problema*
produce *las frutas y verduras;*
~ **store** *la frutería y verdulería*
prohibit *v prohibir*

pronounce *v pronunciar*
public *el público*
pull *v* **(door sign)** *jalar*
purse *el bolso*
push *v* **(door sign)** *empujar;*
　~chair [BE] *el coche de niño*

Q

quality *la calidad*
question *la pregunta*
quiet *tranquilo*

R

racetrack *la pista de carreras*
racket (sports) *la raqueta*
railway station [BE] *la estación del tren*
rain *la lluvia;*
　~ coat *el impermeable;*
　~ forest *el bosque pluvial;*
　~ y *lluvioso*
rap (music) *el rap*
rape *v violar;*
　~n *la violación*
rash *el salpullido*
razor blade *la hoja de afeitar*
reach *v localizar*
ready *listo*
real *auténtico*
receipt *el recibo*
receive *v recibir*
reception *la recepción*
recharge *v recargar*

recommend *v recomendar*
recommendation
　la recomendación
recycle *v reciclar*
refrigerator *el refrigerador*
region *la región*
registered mail *el correo certificado*
regular *normal*
relationship *la relación*
rent *v rentar*
rental car *el auto rentado*
repair *v arreglar*
repeat *v repetir*
reservation *la reserva;*
　~ desk *la taquilla*
reserve *v reservar*
restaurant *el restaurante*
restroom *el sanitario*
retired *jubilado*
return *v (something) devolver;*
　~ n [BE](trip) *redondo*
rib (body part) *la costilla*
right (direction) *derecha;*
　~ of way *derecho de paso*
ring *el anillo*
river *el río*
road map *el mapa de carreteras*
rob *robar*
robbed *robado*
romantic *romántico*

room *la habitación;*
 ~ key *la llave de habitación;*
 ~ service
 el servicio al cuarto
round-trip *viaje redondo*
route *la ruta*
rowboat *el bote de remos*
rubbish [BE] *la basura;*
 ~ bag [BE]
 la bolsa de basura
rugby *el rubgy*
ruins *las ruinas*
rush *la prisa*

S

sad *triste*
safe *n la caja fuerte;*
 ~ adj *seguro*
sales tax *el IVA*
same *mismo*
sandals *las sandalias*
sanitary napkin *la toalla sanitaria*
saucepan *la cacerola*
sauna *el sauna*
save *v (computer) guardar*
savings (account) *la cuenta de ahorros*
scanner *el escáner*
scarf *la bufanda*
schedule *v programar;*
 ~ n *el horario*
school *la escuela*

scissors *las tijeras*
sea *el mar*
seat *el asiento*
security *la seguridad*
see *v ver*
self-service *el autoservicio*
sell *v vender*
seminar *el seminario*
send *v enviar*
senior citizen *anciano*
separated (marriage)
 -separado
serious *serio*
service (in a restaurant)
 el servicio
**sexually transmitted disease
 (STD)** *la enfermedad venérea*
shampoo *el champú*
sharp *afilado*
shaving cream *la crema para afeitar*
sheet *la sábana*
ship *v enviar*
shirt *la camisa*
shoe store *la zapatería*
shoes *los zapatos*
shop *v comprar*
shopping *ir de compras;*
 ~ area *la zona de compras;*
 ~ centre [BE] *el centro comercial;*
 ~ mall *el centro comercial*

short *corto;*
~ **sleeves** *las mangas cortas;*
~ **s** *los pantalones cortos;*
~**-sighted [BE]** *miope*
shoulder *el hombro*
show *v enseñar*
shower *la regadera*
shrine *el santuario*
sick *enfermo*
side *el lado;*
~ **dish** *la guarnición;*
~ **effect** *el efecto secundario;*
~ **order** *la guarnición*
sightsee *v hacer turismo*
sightseeing tour *el recorrido turístico*
sign *v (name) firmar*
silk *la seda*
silver *la plata*
single (unmarried) *soltero;*
~ **bed** *la cama individual;*
~ **room** *una habitación individual*
sink *el lavabo*
sister *la hermana*
sit *v sentarse*
size *la talla*
skin *la piel*
skirt *la falda*
sleep *v dormir;*
~ **er car** *vagón dormitorio;*
~ **ing bag** *el saco de dormir*

slice *v cortar en rodajas*
slippers *las pantuflas*
slow *despacio*
slowly *despacio*
small *chico*
smoke *v fumar*
smoking (area) *área de fumadores*
snack bar *la cafetería*
sneakers *los tenis*
snorkeling equipment *el equipo de esnórquel*
soap *el jabón*
soccer *el fútbol*
sock *el calcetín*
some *alguno*
soother [BE] *el chupón*
sore throat *garganta irritada*
sorry *lo siento*
south *el sur*
souvenir *el recuerdo;*
~ **store** *la tienda de recuerdos*
spa *spa*
Spanish *el español*
spatula *la espátula*
speak *v hablar*
special (food) *la especialidad de la casa*
specialist (doctor) *el especialista*
specimen *el ejemplar*
speeding *el exceso de velocidad*
spell *v deletrear*

spicy *picante*
spine (body part) *la columna vertebral*
spoon *la cuchara*
sports *los deportes;*
  ~ massage *el masaje deportivo*
sporting goods store *la tienda de artículos deportivos*
sprain *el esguince*
square *cuadrado;*
  ~ kilometer *el kilómetro cuadrado;*
  ~ meter *el metro cuadrado*
stadium *el estadio*
stairs *las escaleras*
stamp *v* **(a ticket)** *marcar;*
  ~ *n* **(postage)** *la estampilla*
start *v empezar*
starter [BE] *el aperitivo*
station *la estación;*
  bus ~ *la estación de camiones;*
  gas ~ *la gasolinera;*
  petrol ~ [BE] *la gasolinera;*
  railway ~ [BE]
  la estación del tren;
  underground ~ [BE]
  la estación del metro
statue *la estatua*
stay *v quedarse*
steal *v robar*
steep *empinado*
sterling silver *la plata de ley*

sting *la picazón*
stolen *robado*
stomach *el estómago;*
  ~ache *el dolor de estómago*
stop *v parar;*
  ~ *n la parada*
store directory *el directorio de tiendas*
storey [BE] *la planta*
stove *el horno*
straight *de frente*
strange *extraño*
stream *el arroyo*
stroller *la carreola*
student *el estudiante*
study *v estudiar*
studying *estudiando*
stunning *impresionante*
subtitle *el subtítulo*
subway *el metro;*
  ~ station
  la estación del metro
suit *el traje*
suitcase *la maleta*
sun *el sol;*
  ~ block *el bloqueador solar;*
  ~ burn *la quemadura solar;*
  ~ glasses *los lentes oscuros;*
  ~ ny *soleado;*
  ~ screen *el protector solar;*
  ~ stroke *la insolación*

supermarket *el supermercado*
surfboard *la tabla de surf*
surgical spirit [BE] *el alcohol etílico*
swallow *v tragar*
sweater *el suéter*
sweatshirt *la sudadera*
sweet (taste) *dulce;*
swelling *la hinchazón*
swim *v nadar;*
~ **suit** *traje de baño*
symbol (keyboard) *el símbolo*
synagogue *la sinagoga*

T

table *la mesa*
tablet (medicine) *la pastilla*
take *v llevar;*
~ **away [BE]** *para llevar*
tampon *el tampón*
taste *v probar*
taxi *el taxi*
team *el equipo*
teaspoon *la cucharadita*
telephone *el teléfono*
temple (religious) *el templo*
temporary *temporal*
tennis *el tenis*
tent *la tienda de campaña;*
~ **peg** *la estaca;*
~ **pole** *el palo*
terminal (airport) *la terminal*
terracotta *la terracota*

terrible *terrible*
text *v* **(send a message)**
enviar un mensaje de texto;
~ *n* **(message)** *el texto*
thank *v dar las gracias a;*
~ **you** *gracias*
that *eso*
theater *el teatro*
theft *el robo*
there *ahí*
thief *el ladrón*
thigh *el muslo*
thirsty *sediento*
this *esto*
throat *la garganta*
ticket *el boleto;*
~ **office** *la taquilla*
tie (clothing) *la corbata*
time *el tiempo;*
~ **table [BE]** *el horario*
tire *la rueda*
tired *cansado*
tissue *el pañuelo de papel*
tobacconist *la tabaquería*
today *hoy*
toe *el dedo del pie;*
~ **nail** *la uña del pie*
toilet [BE] *el sanitario;*
~ **paper** *el papel higiénico*
tomorrow *mañana*
tongue *la lengua*

tonight *esta noche*
too *demasiado*
tooth *el diente;*
~ **brush** *el cepillo de dientes;*
~ **paste** *la pasta de dientes*
total (amount) *el total*
tough (food) *duro*
tourist *el turista;*
~ **information office**
la oficina de turismo
tour *el recorrido turístico*
tow truck *la grúa*
towel *la toalla*
tower *la torre*
town *la ciudad;*
~ **hall** *el ayuntamiento;*
~ **map** *el mapa de ciudad;*
~ **square** *la plaza*
toy *el juguete;*
~ **store** *la juguetería*
track (train) *el andén*
traditional *tradicional*
traffic light *el semáforo*
trail *la pista;*
~ **map** *el mapa de la pista*
trailer *el remolque*
train *el tren;*
~ **station** *la estación del tren*
transfer *v cambiar*
translate *v traducir*
trash *la basura*

travel *v viajar;*
~ **agency** *la agencia de viajes;*
~ **sickness** *el mareo;*
~ **er's check [cheque BE]**
el cheque de viajero
tree *el árbol*
trim (hair cut)
v cortarse las puntas
trip *el viaje*
trolley [BE] *el carrito*
trousers [BE] *los pantalones*
T-shirt *la camiseta*
turn off *v apagar*
turn on *v encender*
TV *la televisión*
type *v escribir a máquina*
tyre [BE] *la rueda*

U

ugly *feo*
umbrella *el paraguas*
unattended *desatendido*
unbranded medication [BE]
el medicamento genérico
unconscious *inconsciente*
underground [BE] *el metro;*
~ **station [BE]** *la estación del metro*
underpants [BE]
los calzones
understand *v entender*
underwear *la ropa interior*

United Kingdom (U.K.)
el Reino Unido
United States (U.S.) *los Estados
Unidos*
university
la universidad
unleaded (gas)
la gasolina sin plomo
upper *superior*
urgent *urgente*
use *v usar*
username *el nombre de usuario*
utensil *el cubierto*

V

vacancy *la habitación libre*
vacation *las vacaciones*
vaccination *la vacuna*
vacuum cleaner *la aspiradora*
vagina *la vagina*
vaginal infection *la infección
vaginal*
validity *validez*
valley *el valle*
valuable *de valor*
value *el valor*
VAT [BE] *el IVA*
vegetarian *vegetariano*
vehicle registration
los papeles del auto
viewpoint [BE] *el mirador*
village *el pueblo*

vineyard *el viñedo*
visa (passport document)
la visa
visit *v visitar;*
~ing hours *el horario de visita*
visually impaired
la persona con discapacidad visual
vitamin *la vitamina*
V-neck *el cuello en V*
volleyball game *el partido de
voleibol*
vomit *v vomitar*

W

wait *v esperar;*
~ *n la espera;*
~ ing room *la sala de espera*
waiter *el mesero*
waitress *la mesera*
wake *v despertarse;*
~-up call *la llamada
despertador*
walk *v caminar;*
~n *la caminata;*
~ing route *la ruta de
excursionismo*
wall clock *el reloj de pared*
wallet *la cartera*
warm *v calentar;*
~ *adj* **(temperature)** *calor*
washing machine *la lavadora*
watch *el reloj*

water skis *los esquís acuáticos*
waterfall *la cascada*
weather *el tiempo*
week *la semana;*
  ~end *el fin de semana;*
  ~ly *semanal*
welcome *v acoger;*
  ~ *bienvenido*
well *bien;*
  ~-rested *descansado*
west *el oeste*
what (question) *qué*
wheelchair *la silla de ruedas;*
  ~ ramp *la rampa para la silla de ruedas*
when (question) *cuándo*
where (question) *dónde*
white gold *el oro blanco*
who (question) *quién*
widowed *viudo*
wife *la esposa*
window *la ventana;*
  ~ case *el aparador*
windsurfer *el surfista*
wine list *la carta de vinos*

wireless *inalámbrico;*
  ~ internet
  el acceso de Internet inalámbrico;
  ~ internet service *el servicio inalámbrico a Internet;*
  ~ phone *el teléfono inalámbrico*
with *con*
withdraw *v retirar*
without *sin*
woman *la mujer*
wool *la lana*
work *v trabajar*
wrap *v envolver*
wrist *la muñeca*
write *v escribir*

Y

year *el año*
yellow gold *el oro amarillo*
yes *sí*
yesterday *ayer*
young *joven*
youth hostel *el hostal juvenil*

Z

zoo *el zoológico*

A

la abadía *abbey*

el abanico *fan (souvenir)*

abierto *adj open*

el abogado *lawyer*

abrazar *v hug*

el abrelatas *can opener*

el abrigo *coat*

abrir *v open*

los abuelos *grandparents*

aburrido *boring*

acampar *v camp*

el acantilado *cliff*

el acceso *access;*

  ~ inalámbrico a Internet
wireless internet;

  ~ para discapacitados
*handicapped-[disabled- BE]
accessible*

el accidente *accident*

el aceite *oil*

aceptar *v accept*

acoger *v welcome*

acompañar a *v join*

el acondicionador *conditioner*

la acupuntura *acupuncture*

el adaptador *adapter*

adicional *extra*

adiós *goodbye*

las aduanas *customs*

el aeropuerto *airport*

afilado *sharp*

la agencia *agency;*

  ~ de viajes *travel agency*

agotado *exhausted*

el agua *water;*

  ~ caliente *hot water;*

  ~ potable *drinking water*

el agua de colonia *cologne*

las aguas termales *hot spring*

ahí *there*

ahora *now*

el aire *air;*

  ~ acondicionado *air conditioning*

la alberca *pool;*

  ~ cubierta *indoor pool;*

  ~ exterior *outdoor pool*

algo *anything*

el algodón *cotton*

alguno *some*

alimentar *v feed*

**el allanamiento de
morada** *break-in (burglary)*

la almohada *pillow*

el alojamiento *accommodation*

alto *high*

amable *nice*

la ambulancia *ambulance*

el amigo *friend*
el amor *n love*
el andén *track [platform BE] (train)*
anémico *anemic*
la anestesia *anesthesia*
el anillo *ring*
el animal *animal*
antes de *before*
el antibiótico *antibiotic*
el antro *bar, club*
el año *year*
apagar *v turn off*
el aparador *window case*
el apéndice *appendix (body part)*
el aperitivo *appetizer [starter BE]*
aquí *here*
el árbol *tree*
la aromaterapia *aromatherapy*
arreglar *v repair*
el arroyo *stream*
la arteria *artery*
la articulación *joint (body part)*
los artículos *goods;*
  ~ para el hogar *household good*
la artritis *arthritis*
asaltar *v mug*
el asalto *attack*
el asiento *seat;*
  ~ de pasillo *aisle seat;*
  ~ para niños *car seat;*
asistir *v attend*

asmático *asthmatic*
la aspiradora *vacuum cleaner*
la aspirina *aspirin*
los audífonos *headphones*
Australia *Australia*
australiano *Australian*
auténtico *real*
el auto *car;*
  ~ automático *automatic car;*
  ~ cama *sleeper [sleeping BE] car;*
  ~ con transmisión manual *manual car;*
  ~ rentado *rental [hire BE] car*
automático *automatic*
la autopista *highway [motorway BE]*
el autoservicio *self-service*
la avería *breakdown*
el avión *airplane, plane*
avisar *v notify*
ayer *yesterday*
la ayuda *n help*
ayudar *v help*
el ayuntamiento *town hall*
azul *blue*

B

bailar *v dance*
bajarse *v get off (a train, bus, subway)*
bajo *low*
el ballet *ballet*

el banco *bank*
el baño *bathroom*
barato *cheap, inexpensive*
el barco *boat*
el básquetbol *basketball*
la basura *trash [rubbish BE]*
la batería *battery (car)*
el bebé *baby*
beber *v drink*
la bebida *n drink*
beige *beige*
el béisbol *baseball*
las bellas artes *arts*
besar *v kiss*
el biberón *baby bottle*
la biblioteca *library*
la bicicleta *bicycle;*
  ~ de montaña *mountain bike*
bienvenido *welcome*
el billete *n bill (money)*
el bikini *bikini*
blanco *white*
el bloqueador solar *sunscreen*
la blusa *blouse*
la boca *mouth*
el boleto *ticket;*
  ~ de ida *one-way ticket;*
  ~ del camión *bus ticket;*
  ~ electrónico *e-ticket;*
  ~ redondo *round trip [return BE]*
  ticket

la bolsa de basura *garbage*
  [rubbish BE] bag
el bolsillo *pocket*
el bolso *purse [handbag BE]*
los bomberos *fire department*
bonito *cute*
borrar *v clear (on an ATM);*
  ~ *v delete (computer)*
el bosque *forest;*
  ~ pluvial *rainforest*
las botas *boots;*
  ~ de montaña *hiking boots*
el bote *jar*
el bote de remos *rowboat*
la botella *bottle*
el brazo *arm*
británico *British*
el broche *brooch*
bucear *to dive*
buenas noches *good evening*
buenas tardes *good afternoon*
bueno *adj good*
buenos días *good morning*
la bufanda *scarf*
el buzón de correo *mailbox*
  [postbox BE]

C

la cabaña *cabin (house)*
la cabeza *head (body part)*
la cacerola *saucepan*
el café Internet *internet cafe*

la cafetería *cafe, coffee shop, snack bar*
la caja *box;*
  ~ de cigarros *carton of cigarettes*
la caja fuerte *n safe*
el cajero *cashier;*
  ~ automático *ATM*
el calcetín *sock*
la calefacción *heater [heating BE]*
calentar *v heat, warm*
la calidad *quality*
calor *hot, warm (temperature)*
las calorías *calories*
los calzones *briefs [underpants BE] (clothing)*
la cama *single bed;*
  ~ matrimonial *double bed*
la cámara *camera;*
  ~ digital *digital camera*
el camarote *cabin (ship)*
el camastro *deck chair*
cambiar *v change, exchange, transfer*
el cambio *n change (money);*
  ~ de divisas *currency exchange*
caminar *v walk*
la caminata *n walk*
el camino *path*
el camión *bus;*
  ~ rápido *express bus*
la camisa *shirt*

la camiseta *T-shirt*
el campamento *campsite*
el campo *field (sports);*
  ~ de batalla *battleground;*
  ~ de golf *golf course*
Canadá *Canada*
canadiense *Canadian*
cancelar *v cancel*
el candado *n lock*
cansado *tired*
el cañón *canyon*
la cara *face*
el carbón *charcoal*
el carnicero *butcher*
caro *expensive*
el carrito *cart [trolley BE] (grocery store);*
  ~ de equipaje *luggage cart*
la carta *letter*
la carta *menu;*
  ~ de bebidas *drink menu;*
  ~ de vinos *wine list;*
  ~ para niños *children's menu*
la cartera *wallet*
la casa *house;*
  ~ de cambio *currency exchange office*
la casa rodante *mobile home*
casado *married*
casarse *v marry*
la cascada *waterfall*

el casco *helmet*
el casillero *luggage locker*
el castillo *castle*
el catarro *cold (sickness)*
la catedral *cathedral*
el catre *cot*
causar daño *v damage*
el CD *CD*
la cena *dinner*
el centímetro *centimeter*
el centro *downtown area;*
  comercial *shopping mall*
  [centre BE];
  ~ de negocios *business center*
el cepillo de pelo *hair brush*
la cerámica *pottery*
cerca *near;*
  ~ de aquí *nearby*
el cerillo *n match*
cerrado *closed*
cerrar *v close, lock;*
  ~ sesión *v log off (computer)*
el certificado *certificate*
la cesta *basket (grocery store)*
el chaleco salvavidas *life jacket*
el champú *shampoo*
chapoteadero *kiddie [paddling*
  BE] pool
la chaqueta *jacket*
el cheque *n check [cheque BE]*
  (payment);

~ de viajero
traveler's check [cheque BE]
el chicle *chewing gum*
chico *small*
chocar *v crash (car)*
el chupón *pacifier [soother BE]*
el ciclismo *cycling*
la ciencia *science*
el cigarrillo *cigarette*
la cima *peak (of a mountain)*
el cine *movie theater*
la cinta transportadora *conveyor*
  belt
el cinturón *belt*
la cita *appointment*
la ciudad *town*
la clase *class;*
  ~ ejecutiva *business class;*
  ~ turista *economy class*
el club de jazz *jazz club*
la cobija *blanket*
cobrar *v bill (charge);*
  ~ *v cash;*
  ~ *v charge (credit card)*
el cobre *copper*
la carriola *stroller [pushchair BE]*
la cocina *kitchen*
cocinar *v cook*
el código *area code*
el código de país *country code*
el codo *elbow*

el colador colander
los cólicos menstruales
  menstrual cramps
la colina hill
el collar necklace
el color color
la columna vertebral spine (body
  part)
el comedor dining room
comer v eat
la comida food, lunch, meal;
  ~ rápida fast food
cómo how
**el compañero de
  trabajo** colleague
la compañía company;
  ~ aérea airline;
  ~ de seguros insurance company
comprar v buy, shop
la computadora computer
con with
el concierto concert
el condón condom
conducir v drive
conectarse v connect (internet)
la conexión connection (internet);
  ~ de vuelo connection (flight)
la conferencia conference
confirmar v confirm
el congelador freezer
la congestión congestion

conocer v meet (someone)
el consulado Consulate
el consultor consultant
contagioso contagious
la contraseña password
el corazón heart
la corbata tie (clothing)
el correo n mail [post BE];
  ~ aéreo airmail;
  ~ certificado registered mail;
  ~ electrónico n e-mail
cortar v cut (hair);
  ~ en rodajas to slice
cortarse las puntas v trim (hair cut)
el corte n cut (injury);
  ~ de pelo haircut
corto short
costar v cost
la costilla rib (body part)
la crema cream;
  ~ antiséptica antiseptic cream;
  ~ de afeitar shaving cream;
  ~ hidratante lotion
el cristal crystal
el cruce intersection
la cruda hangover
cuándo when (question)
cuánto cuesta how much
el cubierto utensil
la cuchara spoon;
  ~ medidora measuring spoon

la cucharadita *teaspoon*
la cuchilla desechable *disposable razor*
el cuchillo *knife*
el cuello *neck;*
~ **en V** *V-neck;*
~ **redondo** *crew neck*
la cuenta *account;*
~ **corriente** *checking [current BE] account;*
~ **de ahorros** *savings account*
cuero *leather*
la cueva *cave*
el cumpleaños *birthday*
la cuna *crib*
la curita *bandage*

D

dar *to give;*
~ **fuego** *light (cigarette);*
~ **las gracias a** *v thank;*
~ **pecho** *breastfeed*
de *from, of;*
~ **acuerdo** *OK;*
~ **la mañana** *a.m.;*
~ **la tarde** *p.m.;*
~ **la zona** *local*
declarar *v declare*
el dedo *finger;*
~ **del pie** *toe*
de frente *straight*
deletrear *v spell*

delicioso *delicious*
la dentadura *denture*
el dentista *dentist*
dentro *in*
el departamento *apartment*
la depilacion *wax;*
~ **de cejas** *eyebrow wax;*
~ **de las ingles** *bikini wax*
deportes *sports*
depositar *v deposit*
el depósito bancario *deposit (bank)*
la derecha *right (direction)*
el derecho de paso *right of way*
desaparecido *missing*
desatendido *unattended*
el desayuno *breakfast*
descansado *well-rested*
desconectar *v disconnect (computer)*
el descuento *discount*
desechable *disposable*
el desierto *desert*
el desodorante *deodorant*
despacio *slowly*
despertarse *v wake*
después *after*
el destapador *bottle opener*
el destapador *plunger*
el detergente *detergent*
detrás de *behind (direction)*

devolver *v exchange, return (goods)*
el día *day*
diabético *diabetic*
el diamante *diamond*
la diarrea *diarrhea*
el diente *tooth*
el diésel *diesel*
difícil *difficult*
digital *digital*
el dinero *money*
la dirección *address;*
~ **de correo electrónico**
e-mail address
discapacitado *handicapped*
[disabled BE]
la discoteca *club (dance, night);*
~ **gay** *gay club*
disculparse *v excuse (to get*
attention)
disfrutar *v enjoy*
disponible *available*
divorciar *v divorce*
doblado *dubbed*
doblando (la esquina) *around*
(the corner)
la docena *dozen*
el doctor *doctor*
la documentación *check-in*
(airport)
documentar *check (luggage)*
el dólar *dollar (U.S.)*

el dolor *pain;*
~ **de cabeza** *headache;*
~ **de espalda** *backache;*
~ **de estómago** *stomachache;*
~ **de oído** *earache;*
~ **de pecho** *chest pain*
dónde *where (question)*
dormir *v sleep*
el dormitorio *dormitory*
dulce *sweet (taste)*
durante *during*
el DVD *DVD*

E

la edad *age*
el edificio *building*
el efectivo *cash*
el efecto secundario *side effect*
el ejemplar *specimen*
el elevador *elevator [lift BE]*
embarazada *pregnant*
embarcar *v board*
empezar *v begin, start*
empinado *steep*
empujar *v push (door sign)*
en la esquina *on the corner*
el encaje *lace*
el encendedor *lighter*
encender *v turn on*
el enchufe *electric outlet*
la enfermedad venérea
sexually transmitted disease (STD)

el enfermero/la enfermera *nurse*
enfermo *sick*
enseñar *v show*
entender *v understand*
la entrada *admission/cover charge;*
~ **entrance**
entrar *v enter*
el entretenimiento *entertainment*
enviar *v send, ship;*
~ **por correo** *v mail;*
~ **un correo electrónico** *v*
e-mail; ~ **un fax** *v fax;*
~ **un mensaje de texto**
v text (send a message)
envolver *v wrap*
la época *period (of time)*
el equipaje *luggage [baggage BE];*
~ **de mano** *carry-on (piece of*
hand luggage)
el equipo *team; equipment;*
~ **de buceo** *diving equipment;*
~ **de esnórquel** *snorkeling*
equipment
el error *mistake*
las escaleras *stairs;*
~ **eléctricas** *escalators*
el escáner *scanner*
la escoba *broom*
escribir *v write;*
~ **a máquina** *v type*
la escuela *school*

el esguince *sprain*
el esmalte *enamel (jewelry)*
eso *that*
la espalda *back*
el español *Spanish*
la espátula *spatula*
la especialidad de la casa *special*
(food)
el especialista *specialist (doctor)*
la espera *n wait*
esperar *v wait*
los esquís acuáticos *water skis*
esta noche *tonight*
la estaca *tent peg*
la estación *station;*
~ **de camiones** *bus station;*
~ **del metro** *subway*
[underground BE] station;
~ **de policía** *police station*
~ **del tren** *train [railway BE]*
station
el estacionamiento
parking garage;
~ *parking lot [car park BE]*
estacionar *v park*
el estadio *stadium*
el estado de salud *condition*
(medical)
los Estados Unidos
United States (U.S.)
estadounidense *American*

la estampilla *n* stamp (postage)
el estanque *pond*
estar *v* be
la estatua *statue*
el este *east*
el estilista *hairstylist*
esto *this*
el estómago *stomach*
estreñido *constipated*
el estuche para la cámara
   camera case
estudiando *studying*
estudiar *v* study
la estufa *stove*
la estufa portátil *camp stove*
el euro *euro*
el exceso *excess;*
   ~ **de velocidad** *speeding*
la excursión *excursion*
el excusado químico *chemical*
   toilet
experto *expert (skill level)*
la extensión *extension (phone)*
extra grande *extra large*
extraer *v* extract (tooth)
extraño *strange*

F

el facial *facial*
fácil *easy*
la factura *bill [invoice BE]*
la falda *skirt*

la familia *family*
la farmacia *pharmacy [chemist BE]*
el fax *n* fax
la fecha *date (calendar)*
feliz *happy*
feo *ugly*
la fianza *deposit (to reserve a room)*
la fiebre *fever*
el fin de semana *weekend*
firmar *v* sign (name)
la flor *flower*
el foco *lightbulb*
la fórmula *formula (baby)*
el formulario *form*
la foto *exposure (film);*
   ~ *photo;*
   ~ **digital** *digital photo;*
   ~ **copia** *photocopy;*
   ~ **grafía** *photography*
los frenos *brakes (car)*
frente a *opposite*
fresco *fresh*
frío *cold (temperature)*
las frutas y verduras *produce*
la frutería y verdulería
   produce store
el fuego *fire*
la fuente *fountain*
fuera *outside*
el fuerte *fort*
fumar *v* smoke

el fútbol *soccer [football BE]*

G

el garaje *garage (parking)*
la garganta *throat*
la garganta irritada *sore throat*
el gas butano *cooking gas*
la gasolina *gas [petrol BE];*
  ~ sin plomo *unleaded gas*
la gasolinera *gas [petrol BE] station*
gay *gay*
el gel *gel (hair)*
el gerente *manager*
el gimnasio *gym*
el ginecólogo *gynecologist*
la gota *drop (medicine)*
grabar *v burn (CD);*
  ~ *v engrave*
gracias *thank you*
los grados *degrees (temperature);*
  ~ centígrado *Celsius*
el gramo *gram*
grande *large*
la granja *farm*
gratuito *free*
gris *gray*
la grúa *tow truck*
el grupo *group*
guapo *attractive*
guardar *v save (computer)*
la guarnición *side dish, order*
el guía *guide*

la guía *guide book;*
  ~ de tiendas *store directory*
gustar *v like;*
me gusta *I like*

H

la habitación *room;*
  ~ libre *vacancy;*
  ~ sencilla *single room*
hablar *v speak*
hacer *v do;*
  ~ una apuesta *v place (a bet);*
  ~ un arreglo *v alter;*
  ~ una llamada *v phone;*
  ~ las maletas *v pack;*
  ~ turismo *sightseeing*
hambriento *hungry*
helado *adj frozen*
la hermana *sister*
el hermano *brother*
el hielo *ice*
el hígado *liver (body part)*
la hinchazón *swelling*
hipermétrope *far-sighted [long-sighted BE]*
el hipódromo *horsetrack*
el hockey *hockey;*
  ~ sobre hielo *ice hockey*
la hoja de afeitar *razor blade*
hola *hello*
el hombre *man*
el hombro *shoulder*

hondo *deep*
la hora *hour*
el horario *n schedule [timetable BE]*
los horarios *hours;*
  ~ de atención al público
  business hours;
  ~ de oficina *office hours;*
  ~ de visita *visiting hours*
las horas de consulta *office hours*
  (doctor's)
el horno *oven*
el hospital *hospital*
el hostal *hostel;*
  ~ juvenil *youth hostel*
el hotel *hotel*
hoy *today*
el hueso *bone*

I

el ibuprofeno *ibuprofen*
la identificación *identification*
la iglesia *church*
el impermeable *raincoat*
impresionante *stunning*
imprimir *v print*
el impuesto *duty (tax)*
incluir *v include*
inconsciente *unconscious*
increíble *amazing*
la infección vaginal *vaginal*
  infection
infectado *infected*

el inglés *English*
iniciar sesión *v log on (computer)*
el insecto *bug*
insípido *bland*
la insolación *sunstroke*
el insomnio *insomnia*
la insulina *insulin*
interesante *interesting*
internacional
  international (airport area)
el Internet *internet*
el intérprete *interpreter*
el intestino *intestine*
intolerante *intolerant;*
  ~ a la lactosa *lactose intolerant*
introducir *v insert*
ir a *v go (somewhere)*
ir de compras *v go shopping*
Irlanda *Ireland*
irlandés *Irish*
el IVA *sales tax [VAT BE]*
la izquierda *left (direction)*

J

el jabón *soap*
jalar *v pull (door sign)*
el jardín botánico *botanical garden*
la jarra *carafe*
el jazz *jazz*
los jeans *jeans*
joven *young*
las joyas *jewelry*

la joyería *jeweler's*
jubilado *retired*
jugar *v play*
el juguete *toy*

K

el kilo *kilo;*
  ~ gramo *kilogram;*
  ~ metraje *mileage*
el kilómetro *kilometer;*
  ~ cuadrado *square kilometer*

L

el labio *lip*
la laca *hairspray*
el ladrón *thief*
el lago *lake*
la lana *wool*
la lancha motora *motor boat*
largo *long*
el lavabo *sink*
la lavadora *washing machine*
la lavandería *laundromat*
  [launderette BE]
lavar *v wash*
lavar la ropa *laundry*
el lavaplatos *dishwasher*
la lección *lesson*
lejos *far*
la lengua *tongue*
la lente *lens*
los lentes *glasses;*
  ~ de contacto *contact lenses;*

~ oscuros *sunglasses*
las libras esterlinas *pounds*
  (British sterling)
libre de impuestos *duty-free*
la librería *bookstore*
el libro *book*
la lima de uñas *nail file*
limpiar *v clean*
limpio *adj clean*
la línea *line (train)*
el lino *linen*
la linterna *flashlight*
el líquido *liquid;*
  ~ de lentes de contacto
  contact lens solution;
  ~ lavaplatos *dishwashing liquid*
listo *ready*
la litera *berth*
el litro *liter*
la llamada *n call;*
  ~ de teléfono *phone call;*
  ~ despertador *wake-up call*
llamar *v call*
la llanta *tire [tyre BE];*
  ~ ponchada *flat tire [tyre BE]*
la llave *key;*
  ~ de habitación *room key;*
  ~ electrónica *key card*
el llavero *key ring*
las llegadas *arrivals (airport)*
llegar *v arrive*

llenar *v fill*
llevar *v take;*
  ~ en auto *lift (to give a ride)*
la lluvia *rain*
lluvioso *rainy*
lo siento *sorry*
localizar *v reach*
la loción para después de afeitar *aftershave*
la luz *light (overhead)*

M

la madre *mother*
magnífico *magnificent*
el malestar estomacal *upset stomach*
la maleta *bag, suitcase*
la mandíbula *jaw*
las mangas cortas *short sleeves*
las mangas largas *long sleeves*
el manicure *manicure*
la mano *hand*
mañana *tomorrow;*
  la ~ *morning*
el mapa *map;*
  ~ de carreteras *road map;*
  ~ de ciudad *town map;*
  ~ de la pista *trail [piste BE] map*
el mar *sea*
marcar *v dial*
mareado *dizzy*
el mareo *motion [travel BE] sickness*

el marido *husband*
el martillo *hammer*
más *more*
el masaje *massage;*
  ~ deportivo *sports massage*
el mecánico *mechanic*
la media hora *half hour*
mediano *medium (size)*
la medianoche *midnight*
el medicamento *medicine*
medio *half;*
  ~ kilo *half-kilo;*
  ~ día *noon [midday BE]*
medir *v measure (someone)*
mejor *best*
menos *less*
el mensaje *message;*
  ~ instantáneo *instant message*
el mercado *market*
el mes *month*
la mesa *table*
la mesera *waitress*
el mesero *waiter*
el mesón *bed and breakfast*
el metro *subway [underground BE]*
el metro cuadrado *square meter*
México *Mexico*
mexicano *Mexican*
la mezclilla *denim*
la mezquita *mosque*
el microondas *microwave*

migración *passport control*
el minibar *mini-bar*
el minuto *minute*
el mirador *overlook [viewpoint BE]*
  (scenic place)
mirar *v look*
la misa *mass (church service)*
mismo *same*
los mocasines *loafers*
la mochila *backpack*
el módulo de información
  information desk
molestar *v bother*
la moneda *coin, currency*
la montaña *mountain*
el monumento conmemorativo
  memorial (place)
mostrar *v display*
la moto acuática *jet ski*
la motocicleta *motorcycle*
la motoneta *moped*
el mousse para el pelo *mousse*
  (hair)
movilidad *mobility*
la mujer *wife, woman*
la multa *fine (fee for breaking law)*
la muñeca *doll; ~ wrist*
el músculo *muscle*
el museo *museum*
la música *music;*
  ~ clásica *classical music;*

  ~ folclórica *folk music;*
  ~ pop *pop music*
el muslo *thigh*

N

nacional *domestic*
la nacionalidad *nationality*
nada *nothing*
nadar *v swim*
las nalgas *buttocks*
naranja *orange (color, fruit)*
la nariz *nose*
necesitar *v need*
los negocios *business*
nevado *snowy*
el nieto *grandchild*
la niña *girl*
la niñera *babysitter*
el niño *boy, child*
el nivel intermedio *intermediate*
no *no*
la noche *evening, night*
el nombre *name;*
  ~ de usuario *username*
normal *regular*
las normas de vestimenta *dress*
  code
el norte *north*
la novia *girlfriend*
el novio *boyfriend*
el número *number;*
  ~ de fax *fax number;*

**~ de identificación personal
(NIP)** *personal identification
number (PIN);*

~ de licencia de conducir
driver's license number;

~ de teléfono *phone number;*

~ de teléfono de información
information (phone)

O

la obra de teatro *n play (theater)*
el oculista *optician*
el oeste *west*
la oficina *office;*

  ~ de correos *post office;*

  ~ de objetos perdidos
lost and found;

  ~ de turismo *tourist information
office*

el ojo *eye*
la olla *pot*
la ópera *opera*
la oreja *ear*
la orina *urine*
el oro *gold;*

  ~ amarillo *yellow gold;*

  ~ blanco *white gold*

la orquesta *orchestra*
oscuro *dark*
el otro camino *alternate route*
la oxígenoterapia *oxygen
treatment*

P

padecer del corazón *heart
condition*
el padre *father*
pagar *v pay*
el pájaro *bird*
el palacio *palace;*

  ~ de justicia *parliament building*

los palitos chinos *chopsticks*
el palo *tent pole*
la panadería *bakery*
los pantalones *pants [trousers BE];*

  ~ cortos *shorts*

las pantuflas *slippers*
el pañal *diaper [nappy BE]*
el pañuelo de papel *tissue*
el papel *paper;*

  ~ de aluminio *aluminum
[kitchen BE] foil;*

  ~ higiénico *toilet paper*

el paquete *package*
para *for;*

  ~ llevar *to go [take away BE];*

  ~ no fumadores *non-smoking*

el paracetamol
acetaminophen [paracetamol BE]
la parada *n stop;*

  ~ del camión *bus stop*

el paraguas *umbrella*
pararse *v stop*
el parque *park;*

~ de diversiones *amusement park*
la parrillada *barbecue*
el partido *game;*
  ~ de fútbol *soccer [football BE];*
  ~ de voleibol *volleyball game*
el pasajero *passenger;*
  ~ con boleto *ticketed passenger*
el pasaporte *passport*
el pasillo *aisle*
la pasta de dientes *toothpaste*
la pastelería *pastry shop*
la pastilla *tablet (medicine)*
el patio de recreo *playground*
el peatón *pedestrian*
el pecho *chest (body part)*
el pediatra *pediatrician*
el pedicure *pedicure*
pedir *v order*
el peinado *hairstyle*
el peine *comb*
la película *movie*
peligroso *dangerous*
el pelo *hair*
la peluquería *barber*
los pendientes *earrings*
el pene *penis*
la penicilina *penicillin*
perder *v lose (something)*
perdido *lost*
el perfume *perfume*

el periódico *newspaper*
la periquera *highchair*
la perla *pearl*
permitir *v allow, permit*
el perro guía *guide dog*
la persona con discapacidad visual *visually impaired person*
pesos *pesos (Mexican currency)*
el pewter *pewter*
la picadura de insecto *insect bite*
picante *spicy*
picar *v stamp (a ticket)*
la picazón *sting*
el pie *foot*
la piel *skin*
la pierna *leg*
la pieza *part (for car)*
la pijama *pajamas*
la pila *battery*
la píldora *pill (birth control)*
la pista *trail [piste BE]*
la pista de carreras *racetrack*
la pizzería *pizzeria*
el placer *pleasure*
la plancha *n iron (clothes)*
planchar *v iron*
la planta *floor [storey BE];*
  ~ baja *ground floor*
el plástico transparente *plastic wrap [cling film BE]*

la plata *silver;*
  ~ de ley *sterling silver*
el platino *platinum*
el plato *dish (kitchen);*
  ~ principal *main course*
la playa *beach*
la plaza *town square*
la pluma *pen*
la policía *police*
la pomada *cream (ointment)*
ponerse en contacto con *v contact*
por *for;*
  ~ *per;*
  ~ día *per day;*
  ~ favor *please;*
  ~ hora *per hour;*
  ~ la noche *overnight;*
  ~ noche *per night;*
  ~ semana *per week*
la porción *portion;*
  ~ para niños *children's portion*
el postre *dessert*
el precio *price*
precioso *beautiful*
la pregunta *question*
presentar *v introduce*
la presión arterial *blood pressure*
la primera clase *first class*
primero *first*
los principales sitios de interés
  main attraction

principiante *beginner, novice*
  (skill level)
la prisa *rush*
el probador *fitting room*
probar *v taste*
el problema *problem*
el producto *good;*
  ~ de limpieza *cleaning product*
programar *v schedule*
prohibir *v prohibit*
el pronóstico *forecast*
pronunciar *v pronounce*
provisional *temporary*
próximo *next*
el público *public*
el pueblo *village*
el puente *bridge*
la puerta *gate (airport);*
  ~ *door;*
  ~ de incendios *fire door*
el pulmón *lung*
la pulsera *bracelet*
el puro *cigar*

Q

qué *what (question)*
quedar bien *v fit (clothing)*
quedarse *v stay*
la queja *complaint*
la quemadura solar *sunburn*
querer *v love (someone)*
quién *who (question)*

el quiosco *newsstand*

R

la rampa para silla de ruedas *wheelchair ramp*

el rap *rap (music)*

rápido *express, fast*

la raqueta *racket (sports)*

la reacción alérgica *allergic reaction*

recargar *v recharge*

la recepción *reception*

la receta *prescription*

recetar *v prescribe*

rechazar *v decline (credit card)*

recibir *v receive*

el recibo *receipt*

reciclar *recycle*

el reclamo de equipaje *baggage claim*

recoger *v pick up (something)*

la recomendación *recommendation*

recomendar *v recommend*

el recorrido *tour;*
  ~ en camión *bus tour;*
  ~ turístico *sightseeing tour*

el recuerdo *souvenir*

el refrigerador *refrigerator*

la regadera *shower*

el regalo *gift*

la región *region*

el registro *check-in (hotel);*

~ del coche *vehicle registration*

la regla *period (menstrual)*

el Reino Unido *United Kingdom (U.K.)*

la relación *relationship*

rellenar *v fill out (form)*

el reloj *watch*

el remolque *trailer*

la renta de autos *car rental [hire BE]*

rentar *v rent [hire BE]*

reparar *v fix (repair)*

el repelente de insectos *insect repellent*

repetir *v repeat*

la reserva *reservation;*
  ~ natural *nature preserve*

reservar *v reserve*

respirar *v breathe*

el restaurante *restaurant*

retirar *v withdraw*

retrasar *v delay*

la reunión *meeting*

revelar *v develop (film)*

revisar *v check (on something)*

la revista *magazine*

el riñón *kidney (body part)*

el río *river*

robado *robbed*

robado *stolen*

robar *v rob*

robar v steal
el robo theft
la rodilla knee
rojo red
el rollo film (camera)
romántico romantic
romper v break
la ropa clothing;
  ~ interior underwear
rosa pink
roto broken
el rubgy rugby
las ruinas ruins
la ruta route;
  ~ de excursionismo
  walking route

S

la sábana sheet
el sacacorchos corkscrew
el saco de dormir sleeping bag
la sala room;
  ~ de conciertos concert hall;
  ~ de espera waiting room;
  ~ de reuniones meeting room
la salchichonería delicatessen
la salida check-out (hotel)
la salida n exit;
  ~ de urgencia emergency exit
las salidas departures (airport)
salir v exit, leave
el salón room;

  ~ de belleza hair salon;
  ~ de convenciones
  convention hall;
  ~ de juegos de video arcade;
  ~ de manicure nail salon
¡Salud! Cheers!
la salud health
el salpullido rash
el salvavidas lifeguard
las sandalias sandals
sangrar v bleed
la sangre blood
el santuario shrine
el sartén frying pan
la sauna sauna
el secador de pelo hair dryer
la seda silk
sediento thirsty
la seguridad security
el seguro insurance
seguro safe (protected)
el semáforo traffic light
la semana week
semanal weekly
el seminario seminar
el sendero trail;
  ~ para bicicletas bike route
el seno breast
sentarse v sit
sentirse mal v be ill
separado separated (marriage)

ser *v be*
serio *serious*
el servicio *restroom [toilet BE];*
  ~ *service (in a restaurant);*
  ~ **completo** *full-service;*
  ~ **de habitaciones** *room service;*
  ~ **inalámbrico a Internet**
  wireless internet service;
  ~ **de Internet** *internet service;*
  ~ **de lavandería** *laundry service;*
  ~ **de limpieza de habitaciones**
  housekeeping service
la servilleta *napkin*
sí *yes*
el sida *AIDS*
la silla *chair;*
  ~ **de ruedas** *wheelchair;*
  ~ **para niños** *child seat*
el símbolo *symbol (keyboard)*
sin *without;*
  ~ **alcohol** *non-alcoholic;*
  ~ **receta** *over the counter*
  (medication)
la sinagoga *synagogue*
el sitio de interés *attraction (place)*
el sobre *envelope*
el sol *sun*
solamente *only*
soleado *sunny*
solo *alone*
soltero *single (marriage)*

el sombrero *hat*
la somnolencia *drowsiness*
sordo *deaf*
el sostén *bra*
el spa *spa*
el subtítulo *subtitle*
sucio *dirty*
la sudadera *sweatshirt*
el suelo *floor*
el suéter *sweater*
súper *super (fuel)*
superior *upper*
el supermercado *grocery store,*
  supermarket
la supervisión *supervision*
el sur *south*
el surfista *windsurfer*
surtir la receta *v fill [make up BE]*
  prescription

T

la tabaquería *tobacconist*
la tabla *board;*
  ~ **de surf** *surfboard*
la talla *size;*
  ~ **grande** *plus size;*
  ~ **pequeña** *petite size*
el taller *garage (repair)*
el talón de equipaje *luggage*
  [baggage BE] ticket
el tampón *tampon*
la tapadura *filling (tooth)*

la taquilla *ticket office*
tarde *late (time)*
la tarde *afternoon*
la tarifa *fee*
la tarjeta *card;*
 ~ de abordar *boarding pass;*
 ~ de cajero automático
 ATM card;
 ~ de crédito *credit card;*
 ~ de débito *debit card;*
 ~ internacional de estudiante
 international student card;
 ~ de memoria *memory card;*
 ~ postal *postcard;*
 ~ de representación
 business card;
 ~ de seguro *insurance card;*
 ~ de socio *membership card;*
 ~ telefónica *phone card*
el taxi *taxi*
la taza *cup;*
 ~ medidora *measuring cup*
el tazón *bowl*
el teatro *theater;*
 ~ de la ópera *opera house*
la tela impermeable *groundcloth*
 [groundsheet BE]
el teleférico *cable car*
el teléfono *telephone;*
 ~ móvil *cell [mobile BE] phone;*
 ~ público *pay phone*

la televisión *TV*
el templo *temple (religious)*
temprano *early*
el tenedor *fork*
tener *v have;*
 ~ dolor *v hurt (have pain);*
 ~ náuseas *v be nauseous*
el tenis *tennis*
los tenis *sneakers*
la terminal *terminal (airport)*
terminar *v end*
la terracota *terracotta*
terrible *terrible*
el texto *n text (message)*
el tiempo *time;*
 ~ weather la tienda *store;*
 ~ de alimentos naturales
 health food store;
 ~ de antigüedades
 antique store;
 ~ de bebidas alcohólicas
 liquor store [off-licence BE];
 ~ de campaña *tent;*
 ~ de deportes
 sporting goods store;
 ~ de fotografía *camera store;*
 ~ de juguetes *toy store;*
 ~ de música *music store;*
 ~ de recuerdos *souvenir store;*
 ~ de regalos *gift shop;*
 ~ de ropa *clothing store*

las tiendas departamentales department store
las tijeras scissors
la tintorería dry cleaner
el tipo de cambio exchange rate
la toalla towel;
~ **de papel** paper towel;
~ **sanitaria** sanitary napkin [pad BE]
la toallita baby wipe
el tobillo ankle
el torneo de golf golf tournament
la torre tower
la tos n cough
toser v cough
el total total (amount)
trabajar v work
tradicional traditional
traducir v translate
traer v bring
tragar v swallow
el traje suit
el traje de baño swimsuit
tranquilo quiet
el transbordador ferry
el trapeador mop
el tren train;
~ **rápido** express train
triste sad
el trozo piece

el turista tourist

U

último last
la universidad university
uno one
la uña nail;
~ **del dedo** fingernail;
~ **del pie** toenail
la urgencia emergency
urgente urgent
usar v use

V

las vacaciones vacation [holiday BE]
vaciar v empty
la vacuna vaccination
la vagina vagina
la validez validity
valioso valuable
el valle valley
el valor value
el vaso glass (drinking)
vegetariano vegetarian
la vejiga bladder
vender v sell
el veneno poison
venir v come
la ventana window
el ventilador fan (appliance)
ver v see

verde *green*

el vestido *dress (piece of clothing)*

el viaje *trip*

viaje redondo *round-trip [return BE]*

el vidrio *glass (material)*

viejo *old*

el viñedo *vineyard*

la violación *n rape*

violar *v rape*

la visa *visa (passport document)*

visitar *v visit*

la vitamina *vitamin*

la vitrina *display case*

viudo *widowed*

vivir *v live*

vomitar *v vomit*

el vuelo *flight;*

~ **internacional** *international flight;*

~ **nacional** *domestic flight*

Z

la zapatería *shoe store*

los zapatos *shoes*

la zona *area;*

~ **de compras** *shopping area;*

~ **para día de campo** *picnic area;*

~ **para fumadores** *smoking area*

el zoológico *zoo*

zurcir *v mend*

Berlitz®

speaking your language

**phrase book & dictionary
phrase book & CD**

Available in: Arabic, Brazilian Portuguese*, Burmese*, Cantonese
Chinese, Croatian, Czech*, Danish*, Dutch, English, Filipino, Finnish*, French,
German, Greek, Hebrew*, Hindi*, Hungarian*, Indonesian, Italian, Japanese,
Korean, Latin American Spanish, Malay, Mandarin Chinese, Mexican Spanish,
Norwegian, Polish, Portuguese, Romanian*, Russian, Spanish, Swedish, Thai,
Turkish, Vietnamese
*Book only